DUNKIRK 1940

The 'miracle' of Dunkirk is one of the most inspiring stories of all time. The British Expeditionary Force had been all but surrounded, and, with the French armies collapsing on all sides, it appeared that Britain was about to suffer the heaviest defeat in its history.

When Winston Churchill's War Cabinet finally accepted that the Battle of France had been lost, preparations were made to try and rescue as many soldiers as possible from the only port left open on the Channel coast of northern France – Dunkirk. As the Allied troops fought desperately to hold back the powerful German divisions, it was estimated that only 45,000 men of more than 200,000 front-line troops could be recovered from France and brought back to the UK.

The Admiralty pressed every kind of vessel into service. Royal Navy destroyers and minesweepers, coastal merchant ships, paddle-steamers, ferry boats, tugs, barges and trawlers, in convoys and alone, the ships and boats sailed to France to face artillery, mines, U-boats, enemy torpedo boats and especially the Luftwaffe. Crewed in many instances by civilian volunteers, this armada repeatedly crossed the Channel facing death with every trip.

But as the port of Dunkirk became untenable, the troops had to be taken directly off the beaches and for that only small boats could be used. So the call went out for private yachts and pleasure boats, even little skiffs and cockle boats, which were often towed across to France.

As the French and British armies performed heroics, holding back the Germans, the ships and boats in their hundreds, bombed and blasted by enemy aircraft and artillery, rescued the bulk of the BEF. By the end of Operation *Dynamo* 338,000 soldiers, British, French and Belgian, had been saved to fight again.

Told on a day by day basis, this account of the evacuation reveals how the nation responded to the call for help and, against every prediction, 'miraculously' rescued the British Expeditionary Force.

John Grehan

John Grehan

Editor: John Grehan
Assistant Editor: Alexander Nicoll
Design: Dan Jarman
Executive Chairman: Richard Cox
Managing Director/Publisher: Adrian Cox
Commercial Director: Ann Saundry
Group Editor: Nigel Price
Production Manager: Janet Watkins
Marketing Manager: Martin Steele

CONTACTS
Key Publishing Ltd
PO Box 100, Stamford
Lincolnshire, PE9 1XQ
E-mail: enquiries@keypublishing.com
www.keypublishing.com

Distribution: Seymour Distribution Ltd.
Telephone: 020 7429 4000
Printed by Warners (Midlands) Plc, Bourne, Lincolnshire.

Published by Key Publishing Ltd.
www.britainatwar.com

British and French troops arriving back at a South Coast port during the evacuation. (Historic Military Press)

CONTENTS

BELOW: **A heavily loaded destroyer edges its way into Dover to disembark its cargo of Allied troops during Operation** *Dynamo.* (Courtesy of Pen & Sword Books)

6 PHONEY WAR

They called it the 'Phoney War', the 'Bore War' or the 'Sitskrieg', as the soldiers of the British Expeditionary Force waited impatiently on the Belgian border for the Germans to attack, but there was nothing phoney about the fighting on the Saar front where British troops manned the famous Maginot Line.

14 'THE GREATEST BATTLE OF HISTORY'

The French and British commanders had spent months devising various schemes to be adopted in the event of a German attack. Yet when it came, the Allies were taken by surprise as the enemy launched one of the most effective offences ever executed.

24 DAY 1: 26 May

It was evident that the German penetration into northern France was unstoppable and that the Allies were heading for a catastrophic defeat. Unless the BEF could be evacuated back to the UK, it's army would be annihilated.

34 DAY 2: 27 May

On the first full day of Operation *Dynamo* it was evident that the rate at which the troops were being evacuated was far too slow. The call went out for more ships – big and small.

42 DAY 3: 28 May

The evacuation from Dunkirk was proving painfully slow, but at last, the 'Little Ships' entered the fray.

50 DAY 4: 29 May

In the first days of Operation *Dynamo* only small numbers of men had been rescued but the situation was beginning to change.

58 DAY 5: 30 May

At last the 'Little Ships' were starting to arrive at Dunkirk in large numbers and evacuation from the beaches surpassed that from the harbour and the Mole.

66 DAY 6: 31 May

Against all expectations, the Germans had failed to prevent the evacuation of the BEF but there were still tens of thousands of men waiting on the exposed beaches.

74 DAY 7: 1 June

Aware that the BEF was getting away, the Luftwaffe undertook its largest raids of the campaign.

82 DAY 8: 2 June

It was hoped that this day would see the last troops lifted from the East Mole and the beaches – providing the perimeter held.

90 DAY 9: 3 June

The BEF had been saved to fight another day. But there were still large numbers of French troops at Dunkirk, so the ships and boats were asked to make one final effort.

Unlike the euphoria which had greeted the declaration of war in August 1914, few welcomed the start of another global conflict in September 1939. The memories, and the scars, of the First World War were still too fresh to be forgotten. It was consternation rather than celebration which marked the news that a British Expeditionary Force was crossing the Channel once again to defend France.

This time there was a new factor for the staff of General Headquarters to consider. In 1914 there had been no threat from the air, for the few aircraft available to the enemy were employed only in reconnaissance. Now the Luftwaffe was Germany's most potent weapon, its fighter and bomber types having demonstrated their deadly proficiency in the Spanish Civil War.

Unless the troops could be transported across to France swiftly and secretly, they might never reach the Continent. With the bulk of the German armed forces engaged in Poland, now was the time to ship the troops to France, and the advanced units of the BEF were on the move on 4 September, within twenty-four hours of war being declared.

In addition, rather than transporting the troops across the Channel, it was arranged for them to be shipped further south. Consequently, they were landed at Cherbourg, with their stores and vehicles being despatched to Nantes, St. Nazaire, and Brest. Ahead of the troops were sent units of the Docks and Transportation services and within forty-eight hours of arriving at the French ports, these men, who, in the main, had been recruited from Port Authorities around Britain, had the berths allocated to the BEF operating at maximum capacity.

The current BEF had been formed in 1938 following Germany's annexation of Austria and Hitler's threatened dismemberment of Czechoslovakia. Before Prime Minister Neville Chamberlain secured a deal with Hitler, which gave the German leader a free hand in Czechoslovakia in return for a vague promise that the Führer would make

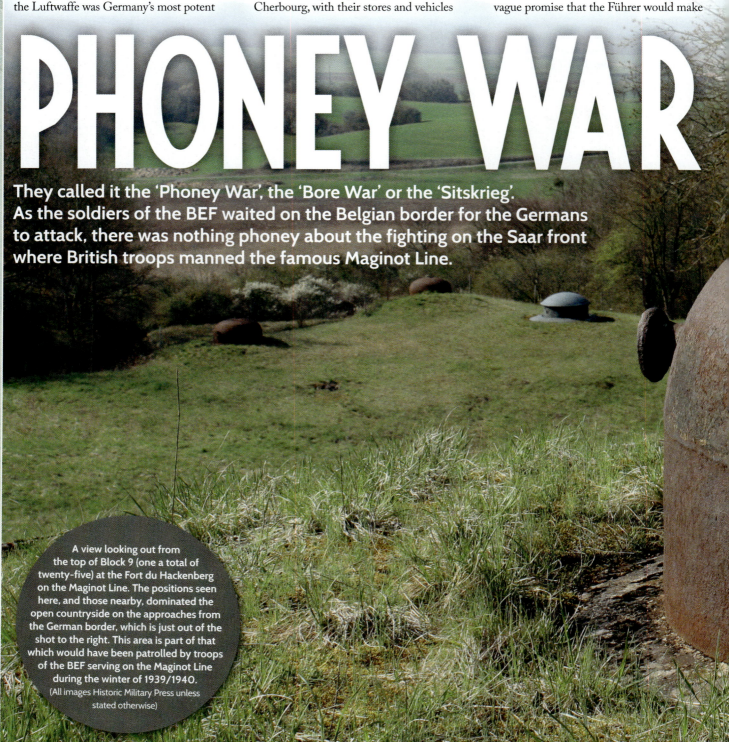

PHONEY WAR

They called it the 'Phoney War', the 'Bore War' or the 'Sitskrieg'. As the soldiers of the BEF waited on the Belgian border for the Germans to attack, there was nothing phoney about the fighting on the Saar front where British troops manned the famous Maginot Line.

A view looking out from the top of Block 9 (one a total of twenty-five) at the Fort du Hackenberg on the Maginot Line. The positions seen here, and those nearby, dominated the open countryside on the approaches from the German border, which is just out of the shot to the right. This area is part of that which would have been patrolled by troops of the BEF serving on the Maginot Line during the winter of 1939/1940.
(All images Historic Military Press unless stated otherwise)

no further territorial demands, it looked as if there would be war in Europe. Though there was a relaxation of tension following the Munich Agreement of 29 September 1938, British and French officers continued to plan for war and for the defence of the French border. This meant that when war finally came plans were already in hand for the deployment of the BEF and within two weeks of the declaration of war in 1939, General Lord Gort VC had already established his headquarters at Le Mans.

As his troops landed, they were passed rapidly through transit camps and their vehicles were cleared at once to Vehicle Marshalling Parks, from where they were despatched in convoys, while the troops themselves left by rail on the same day as they marched off the ships. Since the troops and their vehicles were landed at different ports they had to be collected in an assembly area. The area selected was in the region around Le Mans and Laval, and it took Gort's force around six days to assemble there. Le Mans and Laval are fifty miles apart, the troops being widely dispersed in case of attack by the Luftwaffe. This area is also around 150 miles from the disembarkation ports. Feeding and supplying the troops spread over such distances proved a significant logistical challenge, and the roads and railways of western France were soon choked with traffic.

The British Expeditionary Force's I Corps, commanded by Lieutenant General Michael George Henry Barker, consisted of a headquarters' force and three infantry divisions – the 1st, 2nd and 48th (South Midland) respectively – each of which was composed of three infantry brigades with accompanying artillery and engineers. Under the command of Lieutenant General Alan Brooke, II Corps was similarly composed of three infantry divisions, in this case the 3rd, 4th and 50th (Northumbrian), and the same support arms. Each division also had its own armoured regiment and a machine-gun battalion. ▶

LEFT:
Troops of the British Expeditionary Force on their arrival in France.

BELOW:
HM King George VI visiting a bunker on the Maginot Line, December 1939. Amongst the locations he inspected was Fort du Hackenberg.

It had been originally intended that as soon as it had completed its reorganisation in the assembly area, the BEF should move to a concentration point in the north of France, and remain there in readiness to occupy the line not earlier than 5 October. General Georges decided, however, that it was inadvisable to await the arrival of the whole British Expeditionary Force in the concentration area and expressed a wish that I Corps should move up to the front without delay. Gort agreed and he told Georges that I Corps would take over its sector of the line on 2 October, and that II Corps would follow ten days later.

I Corps began the 250-mile move from the assembly area on 26 September. Tanks, tracked vehicles, and slow moving artillery went by train, with the rest of the Corps advancing on three parallel routes. Three days were allotted for the move of each formation. Two staging areas were arranged on each road, south of the rivers Seine and Somme respectively. With the fear of aerial attack defining the nature of every movement, anti-aircraft guns were set up to defend these river crossings. Luckily, the weather was fine throughout the whole period of the move, and there was little attention from the Luftwaffe.

The first stage of the journey north was 120 miles. An average of 500 vehicles moved daily over each stage of the route, maintaining a distance of 100 yards between each vehicle as a precaution against the constant concern over air attack. A halt of one day

Before the troops could be moved up to the border, the exact sector to be manned by the BEF had to be firmly established. On 22 September Gort received a message from General Alphonse Georges, Commander of the French Front of the North-East, which informed him that his area of responsibility would be from 'Maulde exclusive to Halluin inclusive, and thence a defensive flank along river Lys/Armentières'. To help Gort defend this sector of the line, Georges placed the 51st French Division (Général de Brigade Gillard) under his command. Gort decided to employ it on the left of the sector, covering the towns of Roubaix and Tourcoing.

Troops from the 51st (Highland) Division pass over a drawbridge into Fort de Sainghin on the Franco-Belgian frontier, 3 November 1939. Though this and the other images in the series claim that this shows British troops on the Maginot Line, this is in fact not correct. Built in 1878, Fort de Sainghin was occupied by a garrison and armed with forty-four guns until it was overrun by the Germans in 1914. After the First World War it served as an ammunition depot and did not form part of the Maginot Line. Because of the perceived need for secrecy, the French permitted no photographs of the Maginot Line to be published. In contemporary reports all that was ever allowed were generic drawings. In September 1944, before the Allied advance, the Germans blew up the depot. It was finally decommissioned in 1945.
(Everett Historical/Shutterstock)

The main entrance of the Fort du Hackenberg – the largest fort on the Maginot Line. This fort was the main *gros ouvrage* in the British sector, and in fact was the largest defensive work on the entire Maginot Line. It had a garrison of no less than 1,100 men and forty-three officers and consisted of seventeen 'Battle Blocks' armed with a combination of cannon, howitzers, mortars, grenade-launchers and machine-guns. The whole Hackenberg complex ran for six miles under the hillside that overlooks the village of Veckring.

ABOVE: **A soldier from the Cameron Highlanders, part of the 51st (Highland) Division, looks through a periscope in Fort de Sainghin, 3 November 1939.**

of fortifications to guard France's eastern frontier, using such emotive language as 'concrete is less expensive than a wall of chests.'[1] The Line was built following a national debate, which took place in France after the terrible experience of the First World War, on how to prevent the Germans from invading France in the future. Work began on the Line in 1930. The series of defences ran from the Alps, where the forts defended the border with Italy, along France's eastern frontier until it reached Luxemburg and Belgium.

An advance by the Germans through Luxembourg was discounted because the heavily-wooded Ardennes hills extended along this border region. By contrast, an advance through Belgium, as had happened in 1914, was considered highly likely and France wanted Belgium to participate in this defensive scheme.

But the Belgians did not want to do anything that would compromise their stated position as neutrals. If they would have participated in continuing the Line along their frontier with Germany it would have implied that they viewed the Germans as their enemy – which the Belgian Government feared would provoke an immediate German invasion.

On the other hand, as it was perceived at the time, if France would have stretched the Maginot Line along their border with Belgium, then that small country would have been left with little choice other than to abandon its neutrality and align itself with Germany. So, the northern flank of the magnificent, impenetrable Maginot Line remained open and exposed and it was there where the BEF was deployed – where the main German attack was most likely to be delivered. ▶

for maintenance purposes was made after the first day's move. Nevertheless, I Corps completed its move on schedule, taking over the Maulde-Gruson sector, on the Belgian frontier, from the French. This sector lay between that of the 1st French Army and of the 16th French Corps.

Likewise, II Corps moved into its position on the Belgium border on 12 October. At the same time, General Headquarters was established in and around Habarcq, some eight miles west of Arras.

The BEF was in position ready to face the enemy just five weeks after the declaration of war.

ON THE FRONT LINE

France's main line of defence was, of course, the famous Maginot Line. It was named after the French Minister of War, André Maginot, who secured funding for a series

One of the cupolas on Fort du Hackenberg on the Maginot Line. In December 1939, General Alan Brooke remarked that 'there is no doubt that the whole conception of the Maginot Line is a stroke of genius. And yet, it gave me but little feeling of security, and I consider that the French would have done better to invest the money in the shape of mobile defences such as more and better aircraft and more heavy armoured divisions than to sink all this money into the ground.'

As soon as the British troops arrived on the Belgian border they found that French engineers had already built an almost continuous anti-tank ditch covered by concrete blockhouses equipped with anti-tank guns and machine-guns. It had been agreed earlier that the French engineers would continue to add to these defences in conjunction with the BEF. A massive building programme of reinforced concrete pillboxes and trenches therefore began in earnest. The BEF was digging in.

This saw the start of the 'Phoney War', or the 'Bore War' as it was sometimes called, with the Germans showing no sign of risking an attack upon France or Belgium. As the months passed by with no indication of movement by the enemy, discussions were even held about reducing the strength of the BEF and transferring the troops to other theatres where they would be of more use.

The British, though, were not idle during their time on the Belgian border. So much so, in fact, that by early May 1940 more than 400 concrete pill-boxes and bunkers of varying size had been completed with over 100 more under construction, while work on the improvement of field defences, barbed-wire and other obstacles proceeded continuously on the original front and in the sector north of Armentières recently taken over from the French.

actually undertook an offensive along this sector in 1939 in a bid to draw German troops away from their attack on Poland. However, the French had little interest in provoking the Germans and the operation was called off after just five days. The French troops returned to their positions along the Maginot Line.

Whilst no further large-scale operations took place, the Saar front was not completely quiet. Engagements between the French and the Germans were not uncommon though few risks were taken by either side, the troops being quite content to stay safely within their own lines.

Nevertheless, there were calls for the British troops to take their share of the limited fighting on the Saar and in response to this call the 3rd Brigade of the BEF's 1st Division of I Corps was selected to be the first British brigade to go into the Maginot Line.

Not only was this an opportunity for the men to gain combat experience but it would also counter the German propaganda taunts that 'Britain would fight the war to the last Frenchman'. By putting these troops in the front line, it would show the French just what the British were capable of and help overcome the morale-sapping effects of indefinite inaction in the waterlogged defensive positions on the Belgian border.

This is the impressive retractable turret of one of the Fighting Blocks (No.9) of the Fort du Hackenberg. It was fitted out with two 135mm howitzers. When the turret is retracted the guns are hidden and protected, leaving only the heavily-armoured dome of the turret visible.

LEFT:
British soldiers of the BEF pictured at their post on the front line in France during the cold winter of 1939-1940.

BELOW:
Corporal Thomas William Priday of the 1st Battalion King's Shropshire Light Infantry.
(© The Shropshire Regimental Museum)

Chiefly by the use of excavator machinery, over forty miles of revetted anti-tank ditch had been added to that prepared by the French Army during peace time. Machines had also been used to assist the troops in constructing earthwork defences, in mixing concrete and in burying signal cables.

On either side of the BEF there were French divisions and most of these were no more gainfully employed than their British counterparts, with nothing other than the construction of fieldworks to occupy them. It was only those positioned along the Saar front, ahead of the Maginot Line, that came into contact with the enemy. The French

On 27 November 1939, the 1st Battalion of the King's Shropshire Light Infantry, along with the 1st Battalion Duke of Wellington's Regiment, the 2nd Battalion Sherwood Foresters, and the 3rd Infantry Brigade Anti-Tank Company, were transferred to Metz, before moving up to the Maginot Line itself.

They were now in Lorraine and as the Shropshires' commanding officer pointed out to his men, the older Frenchmen in whose farms and houses they were billeted in had served in the First World War as conscripts for the German Army. Indeed, some people in this border region were still clearly pro-German as the following incident, recorded in the battalion's written history, shows: 'The attitude of some inhabitants was not quite what was expected, for instance an ex-Uhlan NCO deliberately drove his sheep into one of the company billets saying he preferred they should be comfortably accommodated rather than the British troops!'

The Shropshires' first impression of the Maginot Line defences was a mixed one. 'We were all astonished at the "Maginot Line",' wrote one officer. 'As I drove through I hardly noticed anything more than a strong anti-tank obstacle of rails, several strong belts of barbed wire and a few pillboxes, so well were the main forts concealed in our sector. The forts were tunnelled out of a small line of hills. The inside of the forts resembled a battleship, each having engine rooms, living accommodation, kitchen, command post and control rooms, turrets, magazines, hospital and so on.'

ABOVE: **The junction between the main tunnel in Fort du Hackenberg and the branch to the vast underground ammunition stores (on the left).**

ABOVE: **An interior view of the pre-cast steel embrasure of a *Brisant or Avant-poste* (concrete defence post) situated on the *ligne de recueil* near the village of Kirschnaumen.**

The Maginot Line forts could be hermetically sealed against gas attack and access to the Fort du Hackenberg was through this huge anti-blast door. After the fall of France German forces occupied Hackenberg and used it as a factory. In order to get their machines through the narrow gap presented by the door, they had to 'blast' this door aside – the damage caused by this explosion can clearly be seen.

ABOVE: **To transport the troops and supplies rapidly to the fighting blocks at Hackenberg (and in a number of the other forts) electric trains were used. Electricity was delivered from huge diesels via an overhead wire and a trolley attached to the coaches. During his visit to Hackenberg, the King travelled on this railway.**

Another Shropshire officer had quite a different impression of the Maginot Line: 'We were given a lecture by the French divisional commander on the infantry dispositions – the line of contact, the line of "recoil", the line of reserve. In fact, we discovered none of these lines had been prepared in any way – no trenches, no wire, nothing.'

The 3rd Brigade was placed under the command of the French 42nd Division and when the Shropshires moved up to the front the French troops offered the British plenty of advice – but only on how to avoid trouble. This included removing a vital part from each Bren gun just in case someone was stupid enough to fire one at the Germans! The British troops were also advised never to fire at enemy patrols unless they were actually cutting the wire in front of the Allied trenches, just in case the Germans fired back.

Although the French were reluctant to leave the security of the *ligne de contact* (the line of contact), and the most advanced of the Maginot Line's defences, the BEF was there to fight – indeed, the Army's first gallantry medals of the war were won on the Maginot Line. The battalions in the line of contact sent out 'battle' patrols at night to engage the enemy. It was later found that large patrols were difficult to control in the dark and twelve seems to have become established as the best number of men for these missions.

A number of men in each patrol were armed with sub-machine guns, the rest carried grenades, rifles and bludgeons. They blackened their faces, wore cap comforters and long, leather sleeveless Army jerkins. It was, declared one man from another brigade, 'like playing Boy Scouts'.

There was, of course, a serious side to this deadly game of patrol and skirmish, trap and ambush, amongst the deserted houses and empty fields of No Man's Land. It was on one of these patrols that Corporal Thomas William Priday met his death, the first British soldier to die in combat in the Second World War.

'As soon as dark fell the khaki-clad patrols climbed over the parapet and crawled out through the gaps in the wire into the unknown,' ran one report. 'They moved here and there, searched houses and villages whose civilian population had long since been evacuated, ever on the lookout for traces of the passage of their opposite numbers in the German ranks. Always they had to be on the very tip-top of alertness, with hands ready to shoot and eyes keen for the slightest suggestion of a well-placed "booby trap" such as both sides delighted to plant.'

Sadly, it was one of those devices, in fact a British booby trap, which detonated and killed Priday near the small village of Monneren. Some accounts state that he was leading a patrol out, others that the men were returning.

Priday was buried with full military honours. During the ceremony, the French divisional commander gave a long address, saluting Priday as 'Le premier soldat qui est mort pour France'. Unfortunately, the coffin was dropped upside down into the grave with the Union Flag and the accoutrements underneath. Both had to be retrieved and the entire process repeated again from the start.

Following the publication of the BEF's first casualties on 30 January 1940, the French issued a communiqué: 'The British now have their wounded and even their dead, on French soil once again.'

However, the French Prime Minister, Édouard Daladier, was keen to play down the events on the Saar front. 'Military operations have not yet developed with that violence and that vast and brutal extension over wide fronts which they seemed likely to assume,' he told the French National Assembly. 'But we ought not to take this initiative. This war is to us a war for our security and our liberty. Our rule for those who defend us is economy in blood and economy in suffering.'

The economy in lives which the French premier sought certainly seemed valid at that stage of the war when compared with the Great War twenty-five years earlier. Up to December 1939, less than 2,000 British and French Army personnel had lost their lives; by the first Christmas of the First World War that figure had been more than half-a-million. ▶

Deployed to France as part of the BEF, the men of the 2nd Battalion Royal Norfolk Regiment represented 'the first complete infantry unit of the BEF to land in France'. They soon found themselves on the Saar front. Two patrols undertaken on the night of 4/5 January 1940, near the village of Grindoff, resulted in a pair of 'firsts' – one saw the first occasion in which British troops penetrated into German territory, whilst the other led to the award of the BEF's first gallantry medals of the Second World War. Unfortunately these successes were marred by another first for the Norfolks and the BEF – that of losing the first officer in combat. This picture shows Captain Francis Barclay and his men re-enacting the patrol they undertook that led to the gallantry awards – a Military Cross for Barclay and the Military Medal for Lance Corporal H. Davis. The other members of the patrol, Second Lieutenant C.R. Murray Brown, Lance Corporal A. Harris and Lance Corporal A. Spooner, were Mentioned in Despatches. The casualty from the second patrol was Second Lieutenant Patrick Anthony Clement Everitt, the son of Sir Clement and Lady Everitt of Sheringham, Norfolk. Buried with full military honours by the Germans, his body today lies in Rheinberg War Cemetery.

Altogether nine British brigades served on the Maginot Line until, in April 1940, it was decided that the British commitment to the defence of the Line would be increased to divisional strength. The unit chosen for the first – and what would prove to be the last – divisional tour of duty on the Maginot Line was the 51st (Highland) Division.

Commanded by Major General Victor Fortune, the 51st (Highland) Division was a powerful, self-contained formation. It comprised three infantry brigades, the 152nd Brigade (2nd and 4th Battalions Seaforth Highlanders, 4th Battalion Cameron Highlanders), 153rd Brigade (1st and 5th Battalions Gordon Highlanders, 4th Battalion Black Watch) and 154th Brigade (1st Battalion Black Watch, 7th and 8th Battalions Argyll & Sutherland Highlanders), with an Armoured Reconnaissance Regiment of light tanks and Universal carriers, plus three regiments of field artillery and one anti-tank regiment.

To this force were attached another two artillery regiments, two machine-gun battalions and two battalions of Pioneers. General Fortune also had a composite squadron of the RAF under his command, one flight of which were fighters, the other a flight of Westland Lysander Army Co-operation aircraft. The entire force totalled around 21,000 men.

III CORPS

The 51st Division was the first element of what was to become III Corps, which was to be formed in France throughout February and March 1940 as increasing numbers of trained

ABOVE: **Priday was buried in a quiet corner of the small communal cemetery located on the north-eastern outskirts of the village of Luttange. Priday's grave is that on the left; the CWGC headstone beside it is that of 25-year-old Corporal Dennis McGillicuddy of the 2nd Battalion Royal Fusiliers (City of London Regiment) who died on 23 December 1939.**

troops became available. The other two divisions were the 42nd (East Lancashire) and the 44th (Home Counties). With the increase in size of the BEF, so the front line Gort's men would be responsible for was to be similarly extended.

The comparative inactivity which had persisted all through the winter along the Saar front continued during the early days of the 51st Division's occupation of the Line. When the Scots moved up to the *ligne de contact* they found that the French had settled into a comfortable routine of doing nothing that would upset the Germans. When Major James Grant of the 2nd Seaforths suggested a joint patrol against the German lines to his French counterpart, the French officer almost fainted!

Things appeared to change at night, however. 'Punctually at 21.00 hours the fun

began', recalled Sergeant John Mackenzie. 'The whole valley was filled with an ear-splitting volume of sound. Things banged, boomped, screeched, whee-ed, whistled, and thumped. Light flickered from gun-flash and shell-burst. Out in front sped line upon line of tracer, looking like red-hot bees, down and across the valley.' But this drama was an act played out for the generals and the newsreels, the bullets and the shells flying harmlessly over the heads of the men sheltering safely in their trenches. There was no real intention of doing any harm.

Towards the end of April, German patrols became increasingly active against the *ligne de contact*. There was some intense fighting in which the artillery of both sides joined in. Then from the beginning of May this activity died down and an 'uncanny' quiet descended upon the Highlanders' sector.

This period of calm ended on 6 May 1940, when the German artillery shelled the British positions. Then, on 10 May, less than a month after the 51st (Highland) Division had arrived on the Maginot Line, the great German offensive in the West began. In response, the French Commander-in-Chief Général Gamelin issued an 'Order of the Day' at 14.05 hours: 'The attack which we have been anticipating since last October has been launched this morning. It is the beginning of a fight to the death between Germany and ourselves. The watchword for all the Allies is: calm, energy, confidence.'[2]

Within just a few days all confidence had evaporated and panic replaced calm. France was about to suffer its greatest defeat and the BEF faced disaster. ✠

BELOW: **Priday was almost certainly buried in Luttange Communal Cemetery by virtue of the fact that, a short distance down the road is the location of the impressive Château seen here. At the time of his death, and burial, the Château was the location of the Divisional Headquarters for those divisions, either French or British (such as the 51st (Highland) Division in early 1940), that were manning this sector of the Maginot Line.**

NOTES:
1. J.E. and H.W. Kaufmann, *Fortress France. The Maginot Line and the French Defences in World War II* (Connecticut, 2005), p.15.
2. Quoted in Mike Rossiter, *I Fought at Dunkirk* (Bantam Press, London, 2012), p.70.

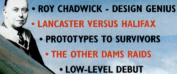

'THE GREATEST BATTLE OF HISTORY'

The French and British commanders had spent months devising various schemes to be adopted in the event of a German attack. Yet when it came, the Allies were taken by surprise as the enemy launched one of the most effective offences ever executed.

Blitzkrieg in action – German troops, including one equipped with a flamethrower, tackle an enemy bunker.
(All images Historic Military Press unless stated otherwise)

On the morning of Friday, 10 May 1940, the Germans launched their predicted invasion of Belgium, and a message was issued from French Headquarters to implement 'Plan D'. This plan called for the BEF to move into Belgium to take up a position on the River Dyle. It meant that the Germans had violated Belgian neutrality, and Britain was treaty-bound to march to her defence.

The formulation of this plan had occupied the minds of Gort and the French commanders, General Georges and General Gamelin, throughout the first months of the war. Between them they had at first decided that, in the event of a German attack, the BEF should continue to hold the frontier defences, pushing forward mobile troops to the line of the River Escaut, while the French 7th Army, on the British left, was to delay the enemy on the line of the Messines Ridge and the Yser Canal. This plan was soon discarded, however, in favour of moving the entire BEF up to the Escaut, where it would hold the line of the river from the point at which it crosses the frontier at Maulde northwards to the neighbourhood of Ghent where the Belgian Army was concentrated. This became known as 'Plan E'.

This plan was also abandoned because, in Gort's words, 'as information became available regarding the defences of the Belgian Army, and its readiness for war, the French High Command formed the opinion that it would be safe to count on the Belgian defence holding out for some days on the Eastern frontier, and the Albert Canal'.

The Belgians had, in fact, been building considerable defensive structures which, though not on the scale of the Maginot Line, were still impressive. It was accepted that the Belgians would be unable to stop the Germans on the frontier, so they decided to build a fortified line in the heart of the country. The time taken for the Germans to advance into Belgium up to the fortified line would allow the army to fully mobilise and dig in – and for Belgium's Allies to come to its help.

The fortified line, then, was intended to run from Antwerp in the north through Leuven and Wavre along the River Dyle, and then on to Namur and Givet (France) along the Meuse. Unfortunately it was incomplete when the Germans attacked, with the vital stretch from Namur to the French border still devoid of fortifications.

Nevertheless, the line of the Dyle was, from the military point of view, a better one than that of the Escaut.

ABOVE: **Destroying bridges was an integral part of the steps taken by the various Allied armies in an effort to disrupt the German advance, temporarily delaying the Blitzkrieg. As this German photograph taken during the offensive shows, it was not just road bridges that were blown up.**

'It was,' Gort explained, 'shorter, it afforded greater depth and its northern portion was inundated, in addition, it represented smaller enemy occupation of Belgian territory'. This latter factor was not merely a political move; the region that would be saved included Belgium's industrial heartland.

What such a move up to the Dyle meant was that the positions on the border which the British and French had been strengthening all winter would be abandoned. It also meant that the moment the Allies were informed of the German invasion of Belgium, the BEF would have to rush some sixty miles up to the Dyle to get there before the Germans and to occupy positions which the troops were unfamiliar with. Of possibly even greater significance

was that this move left a large gap in the Allied front around Gembloux where there was no natural anti-tank obstacle. Earmarked to fill this gap was France's strongest force, the First Army, supported by a full half of its armoured reserves.

So it was that, at approximately 06.15 hours on 10 May, Gort received instructions to put Plan D into effect. He then sent instructions to his corps commanders to begin their move into Belgium at 13.00 hours. 'It was hard to believe,' said Alan Brooke in command of II Corps, 'on a most glorious spring day with all nature looking quite at its best, that we were taking the first step towards what must become one of the greatest battles of history!'[1]

ABOVE: **Two views of a French Char B1 bis tank knocked out during the German advance into France. Nicknamed *Ouragan*, this tank, No.260, was put out of action in the town of Guise which is in the Aisne department to the east of Saint-Quentin.**
(Conseil Régional de Basse-Normandie /US National Archives)

The 12th Royal Lancers, with its Morris CS9 light armoured cars, was the first regiment to cross into Belgium, leading the way to the Dyle through cheering crowds. It reached is destination, unopposed, at 22.30 hours. Everything appeared to be going according to plan, with the French armies on the right and left of the BEF reported as advancing on time.

On the 11th, the bulk of the BEF reached the Dyle on schedule, despite encountering the first of the refugees abandoning their homes ahead of the advancing Germans. But already there was bad news from elsewhere, only one day into the battle. The speed of the German move into Belgium had taken the Belgian Army by surprise and its engineers had failed to demolish important bridges over the Albert Canal and the River Meuse which the Germans were already crossing.

When the French on Gort's right reached their pre-arranged positions, they found that the strong defences the Belgians had boasted of were incomplete and badly sighted. After consultations with General Georges, it was agreed that despite the unexpectedly poor defences, with a few modifications they would continue with Plan D. The Germans, after all, were behaving exactly as anticipated and were marching straight towards the waiting Allied forces – or so it seemed. But just as the Germans were moving into Belgium as expected, the Allied armies had marched into Belgium just as the Germans had expected. The British and French divisions braced themselves for the first clash with the enemy, unaware that they had marched into a trap.

Enemy forces crossing the border into Luxembourg as part of *Fall Gelb*, the codename for the German invasion of the Low Countries, on 10 May 1940. The attack on this small nation began at 04.35 hours that morning; facing only light resistance, Luxembourg was occupied within a single day. Its government escaped to London, where a government-in-exile was formed.

BELOW: **German** *Fallschirmjäger*, **parachute troops, pictured during the attack on Fort Eben-Emael on 10 May 1940. This Belgian fortress occupied a strategic position that dominated several important bridges over the Albert Canal. The fact that these men are not glider-borne would indicate that they were amongst the reinforcement dropped by a number of Junkers Ju 52 transports as the attack on the Belgian fortress continued.**

BOTTOM LEFT: **Two of the armoured cupolas of Fort Eben-Emael. The airborne assault on Fort Eben-Emael, and the three bridges it helped protect, was part of a much larger German airborne operation that involved the 7th Air Division and the 22nd Airlanding Division.**

BOTTOM RIGHT **The main entrance to Fort Eben-Emael today. After the war, General Kurt Student wrote that the operation was 'a deed of exemplary daring and decisive significance'. He added that 'I have studied the history of the last war and the battles on all fronts. But I have not been able to find anything among the host of brilliant actions – undertaken by friend or foe – that could be said to compare with the success achieved by Koch's Assault Group.'** (Courtesy of Guido Radig)

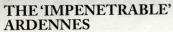

THE 'IMPENETRABLE' ARDENNES

On the 13th, the first skirmishes took place along the British sector, though there was no engagement of any consequence. But some seventy miles to the south of the forward British and French positions there were reports that German forces, having marched through the Ardennes, had crossed the Belgian River Meuse. At this early stage in the unfolding battle the true consequences of this approach by the Germans was not fully appreciated. The French high command considered the densely-wooded and hilly terrain of the Ardennes to be effectively impenetrable to a modern army with all its motorised encumbrances and the line of the River Meuse easily defendable against light forces. This misconception meant that the border along the Ardennes had received comparatively little attention from the French military planners and only a small number of pillboxes and bunkers had been built. To General Gamelin, the French Army's Commander-in-Chief, it simply did not seem worth tying up men and materiel where the Germans could never attack. Gamelin was completely, and catastrophically, wrong.

It was Generalmajor Erwin Rommel's 7th Panzer Division, of Generalleutnant Heinz Guderian's XIX Corps, that led the way over the Meuse supported by the Luftwaffe which carried out the heaviest bombardment of the war to that date and, it is claimed, the most intense the Germans mounted at any stage in the war.

With the BEF and the French First Army holding off the German attacks and the French Second and Third armies manning the Maginot Line and associated areas, now that the panzers were across the river there was little to stop them racing into northern France. All Gamelin's plans and all the preparations the Allies had made were, at a stroke, made redundant. Worse still, was that the vast sums of money and enormous resources that had been sunk into the magnificent Maginot Line had been for nothing, as the German armoured divisions merely swept by its northern flank. The French forces were thrown into chaos.

The following day, 14 May, brought more distressing news for the Allies with the announcement that Holland had been overrun and its government had surrendered. Though this had no immediate effect on the BEF which continued to only be lightly engaged,

the news came as a terrible shock to the Belgians, eroding their already shaky morale.

After breaking through the French 55th and 71st divisions on the Meuse, Guderian's panzers struck and dispersed the hurriedly-formed French Sixth Army at its assembly area west of Sedan. As the panzers continued to move westwards, the French Ninth Army found the Germans had swept round behind its southern flank and almost the entire force surrendered over the next few days– and still the 7th Panzer Division pushed on. Against orders to halt and wait for the rest of XIX Corps and Army Group A to consolidate the ground won, Rommel continued to drive deeper into France. The Belgian, British and French forces in Belgium were in danger of being isolated and cut off from the rest of the French Army.

On 15 May 1940, just five days after the start of the German onslaught, the newly-appointed French Prime Minister, Paul Reynaud, rang his equally recently-installed counterpart in London, Winston Churchill, to announce that: 'We have been defeated. We are beaten; we have lost the battle … The front is broken near Sedan: they [the Germans] are pouring through in great numbers with tanks and armoured cars.'[2] ▷

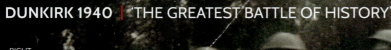

RIGHT:
British soldiers captured during the invasion of France and the Low Countries in 1940 being led off to captivity under guard in Cambrai.

BOTTOM LEFT:
A German self-propelled gun of Panzerjäger SFL Pz.Jg. I on the move through Cambrai during the invasion of France and the Low Countries in 1940.

WITHDRAWAL

At the same time that the French armies were collapsing to the south, Gort was writing that: 'By the night of 15th May the movements envisaged in Plan D were all running ahead of schedule.' That situation was about to change drastically. The French First Army, on the right of the BEF, came under heavy pressure from the German Sixth Army on its front, with the French Ninth Army to its right no longer existing as a fighting force. Général d'Armée Gaston Billotte had no choice but to fall back to the south-west.

Much as in 1914, when the BEF of the First World War was compelled to withdraw from Mons in line with the French withdrawal, so the BEF of the Second World War had to conform to the movements of the French First Army. Likewise, the Belgian Army on the left of the BEF, though not yet seriously engaged, also had to fall back. The decision was taken to revert to Plan E and retreat to the line of the River Escaut. Alan Brooke, saw that the Belgians were 'in a very shaky and jumpy condition' and with the fall of Holland, the Germans would be able to bring an increased number of troops against them. 'The BEF is therefore likely to have both its flanks turned,' he wrote in his diary of 15 May, 'and will have a very unpleasant time in extricating itself out of its current position'.[3]

ABOVE: **Field Marshal John Standish Surtees Prendergast Vereker, 6th Viscount Gort, was given command of the BEF in September 1939. John Gort had fought in the First World War, during which he was Mentioned in Despatches eight times, was awarded the DSO with two Bars and received the Victoria Cross for his actions at the Battle of the Canal du Nord in September 1918.**

On the afternoon of the 16th, Churchill flew to Paris to discuss the deteriorating situation with the French Prime Minister, the Minister for War, Daladier, and Général Gamelin. Gamelin explained that the Germans had pushed sixty miles into northern France, scattering the French armies as they advanced. Churchill, then asked 'Where is the strategic reserve?' Gamelin shrugged his shoulders, and replied with one single word, 'Aucune' – 'none'. The reality was that the French already believed that they had been defeated. The other factor was the speed of the German advance, which baffled the French commanders who were never able to organise a defensive line before the Germans had either pushed through or around them.

Churchill, typically, said that instead of retreating, the Allied armies should counter-attack. Indeed, this was exactly the opinion of Colonel Charles de Gaulle who saw that German communications through Sedan were exposed and vulnerable. On the 17th he led his 4ème Division Cuirassée de Réserve against the German-held village of Montcornet. After some initial success, de Gaulle's attack was driven off. Two days later de Gaulle tried again to cut the German lines of communication, but again failed. At this point, Prime Minister Reynard dismissed Gamelin who had lost his nerve and had accepted that the Allies were beaten. He was replaced by General Maxime Weygand, whose first action was to order an attack on the Germans from both the south and the north. In what became known as the Battle of Arras the British 5th and 50th divisions and the 1st Army Tank Brigade, attacked southwards whilst the 3ème Division Légère Mécanique pushed northwards. Once more, after initial gains, the Germans drove off the counter-attack.

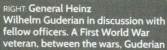

RIGHT: **General Heinz Wilhelm Guderian in discussion with fellow officers. A First World War veteran, between the wars, Guderian became a catalyst for developing a Panzer division in the German Army. By February 1938 he had been promoted to Lieutenant General; later that year Hitler appointed Guderian to the new post of Chief of Mobile Troops. A master of strategy and tactics, he was the officer who led the attack on Poland in September – and in so doing introduced the world to the reality of Blitzkrieg.**

Though the withdrawal to the Escaut was accomplished without too many problems, the failure of the counter-attacks meant that the BEF's rear areas were now under imminent threat. The only British units in these areas were those of the lines of communication troops. It had never been expected that these troops would have to fight, but now every man and every gun was needed to halt the German advance. Amongst the line of communication troops were three infantry divisions – the 12th, 23rd and 46th – which had been stripped of their artillery and heavy equipment and sent over to act as a labour force. These men, some of whom had never even fired their rifles, would have to hold back the full might of the German panzer divisions. They would be almost wiped out, suffering casualties on a scale not seen since the First World War – of the 701 men of the 7th Battalion, Royal Sussex

French gunners in action 'on the Western Front', 29 May 1940.

ABOVE: A contemporary wartime drawing depicting the Fairey Battle crew of Flying Officer Donald Edward Garland in action on 12 May 1940. On this date, Garland's aircraft was one of five from 12 Squadron tasked with targeting bridges over the Albert Canal in an attempt to disrupt the German advance. In the attack that followed, during which the attackers were met by a fierce barrage of anti-aircraft fire, Garland's Battle was shot down.

Regiment, for example, who mustered for duty on the morning of the 20th, just seventy survived to be marched into captivity that night. But crucially, they delayed the Germans for a few hours, and by this date, every hour was precious to the BEF.

THE BATTLE FOR THE SKIES

Attached to the BEF was an Air Component which consisted of nine squadrons of Lysanders and Bristol Blenheims for reconnaissance and army co-operation, along with four squadrons of Hawker Hurricane fighters. In addition to this, the Royal Air Force had despatched to France the Advanced Air Striking Force (AASF) of ten squadrons of light/medium bombers (eight of Fairey Battles and two of Blenheims) and three of Hurricanes. It had also been agreed that if the Germans were to launch an attack a further four squadrons of Hurricanes would be sent to France.

It had been the Battles and Blenheims that had taken on the hazardous, if not suicidal, role of attacking and slowing the advancing German Army. Frequently operating in daylight, usually at low level, and often with meagre or non-existent fighter cover, the attacks took a terrible toll on the Bomber Command aircrews as they faced light and

heavy flak and a formidable Luftwaffe fighter force. By the end of 12 May, the AASF had just seventy-two serviceable bombers. An attempt to bomb the bridges over the Meuse on 14 May to stop the German advance saw the AASF lose a further forty aircraft to Luftwaffe fighters. The French *Armée de l'Air* likewise suffered badly, losing 795 planes in May and June 1940; 320 due to air action, 235 by accidents, 240 on the airfields.

With the Luftwaffe dominating the skies, the French asked Churchill for more fighters. Churchill wanted to support the French as much as possible and he put the request to the War Cabinet. The Prime Minister considered the decision to send more fighters into the battle 'one of the gravest that a British Cabinet had ever had to face'. But as the Germans advanced, the bases of the Air Component and the AASF were in danger of being overrun and the Air Officer Commanding the Air Component was forced to move his headquarters to the UK.

It was clearly unwise, if not impracticable, to send more squadrons over to France, but a number of fighter squadrons were allowed to operate from the UK against the Germans in France. It was Air Chief Marshal Hugh Dowding, Commander-in-Chief of Fighter Command, who stopped Churchill from

committing further aircraft to what was considered a lost cause. He famously wrote to Churchill on 16 May in stark terms: 'I believe that, if an adequate fighter force is kept in this country, if the fleet remains in being, and if Home Forces are suitably organised to resist invasion, we should be able to carry on the war single handed for some time, if not indefinitely. But, if the Home Defence Force is drained away in desperate attempts to remedy the situation in France, defeat in France will involve the final, complete and irremediable defeat of this country.' There is little doubt that Britain's survival in 1940 owed much to Hugh Dowding.

ABOVE: For his actions on 12 May 1940, Garland was posthumously awarded the Victoria Cross, as was Sergeant Thomas Gray – seen here. The citation for these awards noted that, 'much of the success of this vital operation must be attributed to the formation leader, Flying Officer Garland, and to the coolness and resource of Sergeant Gray, who in most difficult conditions navigated Flying Officer Garland's aircraft in such a manner that the whole formation was able successfully to attack the target in spite of subsequent heavy losses'. The third member of Garland's crew, Leading Aircraftman Lawrence Reynolds, did not receive an award.

THE GUARDS' LAST STAND

After repelling the Allied counter-attack at Arras, Rommel pushed on despite reservations from the German High Command, the Oberkommando der Wehrmacht (OKW), that the panzers were too far ahead of the rest of Army Group A. But on 22 May, he was given permission to drive on to the coast and maybe, just maybe, the BEF could be cut off from the Channel ports, and the entire British force surrounded and destroyed.

Though no final decision had been taken regarding abandoning France, the prospect of evacuating the BEF back to the UK had already been seriously considered by the War Cabinet. The only possible ports through which the BEF could be evacuated were Boulogne, Calais and Dunkirk, but with the possibility that the Germans would advance up the coast, it was likely that Boulogne and Calais would be captured. This would leave just Dunkirk open. Nevertheless, if these two ports could be powerfully garrisoned the BEF's southern flank might be secured, or at least the German advance held whilst the main body of the British army was evacuated through Dunkirk.

So, two battalions of the Welsh and Irish Guards, commanded by Brigadier W. Fox-Pitt, sailed for France on the evening of 21 May along with the 275th Battery (less one troop) of the 69th Anti-Tank Regiment. The Guards arrived at Boulogne early the following morning. The port was packed with hordes of panic-stricken refugees desperate to rush on board the British ships, and the Guardsmen had to fix bayonets to clear a path through the mob before they could disembark.

It had not been thought that Boulogne would come under attack and the port had not been provided with a garrison nor had its ancient defences been fortified. Only two days earlier, on 20 May, had the port been provided with any air defence with the deployment of eight 3.7-inch guns of the 2nd Heavy Anti-Aircraft Regiment

ABOVE: **Civilian victims of the Blitzkrieg pictured in Belgium in May 1940.**

ABOVE: **German soldiers repairing war damage in front of the Menin Gate in Ypres following the fighting there in 1940.**

and eight machine-guns of the 58th Light Anti-Aircraft Regiment. These two units were supported by a battery of the 2nd Searchlight Regiment. The only other British personnel at the port were 1,500 men of the Auxiliary Military Pioneer Corps (AMPC), none of whom were equipped as fighting soldiers.

There were a considerable number of young French and Belgian recruits in Boulogne but these had not yet been trained for combat. However, groups of stragglers from the defeated French forces had made their way to the coast and they had salvaged two 75mm guns, two 25mm anti-tank guns and two Renault tanks, one of which was broken down and could only be used on the spot where it stood.[4]

This then was the initial force available for the defence of Boulogne. Heading towards the port was the German 2nd Armoured Division – the panzers were coming.

Scarcely had the Guards taken up their positions when the sound of gunfire from

the south was heard, prompting the men to start 'furiously' digging in. By approximately 17.30 hours, the Germans were within artillery range of the Irish Guards. After a short barrage the panzers attacked but, when the leading tank had been knocked out by one of the Guards' anti-tank guns and the supporting German infantry had been pinned-down, the assault petered out.

The Germans really needed a quick result at Boulogne so that they could press on up the coast to cut off the retreat of the BEF. But there was nothing they could do until dawn the following day. The Guards had already bought Gort's men another day.

At 07.30 hours the following morning, with the panzers in support, the Germans attacked once more. This time the Guards were pushed back and by 10.00 hours they had been forced to withdraw across the railway line which runs close to the River Liane. Three hours later the Irish retreated towards the centre of the town.

ABOVE and BOTTOM (OPPOSITE PAGE): The crew of a Universal carrier watch as refugees pass by on the Brussels to Louvain road, 12 May 1940. (Courtesy of Pen and Sword Books)

LEFT: Lieutenant General Alan Brooke, later Field Marshal Lord Alanbrooke, was in command of the BEF's II Corps and distinguished himself in the handling of his corps during the retreat to Dunkirk. On 29 May he was ordered to return to the UK, being told that he was to be given the task of 'reforming new armies'. In his diary he described his journey back to the coast: 'Congestion on roads indescribable. French army became a rabble and complete loss of discipline. [French] troops dejected and surly and refusing to clear road, panicking every time a Boche plane came over.' Understandably, Brooke had little confidence in the French and, after consulting with General Gamelin, the French commander, he ordered the withdrawal of all remaining British troops from France.

Over to the east the French-held stronghold, the Fort de la Crèche, which defended the coast road about three-quarters of a mile to the north of Boulogne, was taken by the Germans and shortly afterwards the Welsh Guards came under heavy attack. This was the direction in which the reinforcements were supposed to arrive from Calais, so it was now clear to Fox-Pitt that no help would be coming his way. Nor was there much assistance from the French 21st Division, as a large part of this force was attacked and dispersed by Panzers whilst still entrained. Everything then, depended on the Guards. Remarkably, the Guards held on until the 24th, when most of them were taken off by ship. A contingent remained and these held on for another day before surrendering. The next day the evacuation of the BEF began.

'HOLD CALAIS TO THE DEATH!'

Almost all the regular British regiments were with the BEF, but 30 Infantry Brigade was on anti-invasion duties across Suffolk and Kent. On 21 May 1940, at 18.30 hours, instructions were issued for all ranks to report back to camp – immediately. They were on their way to Calais.

Incredibly, by 23.00 hours, the entire brigade was entrained and on its way to Dover. Just a few hours later the 1st Battalion Queen Victoria Rifles arrived at Dover, followed by the 2nd Battalion King's Royal Rifles and the 1st Rifle Brigade. Armoured support took the form of the 3rd Battalion Royal Tank Regiment, equipped with Cruiser Mk.I tanks. The 229th Anti-tank battery of the Royal Artillery completed the force, all of which would be under the command of Brigadier Claude Nicholson.

Nicholson had been instructed to keep open communications between Calais and Boulogne, but it was evident that if he moved any of his troops out of Calais towards Boulogne, then Calais itself would be undefended. So, Nicholson decided to concentrate on defending Calais.

Nicholson now ordered his men to be prepared to hold Calais 'to the last'. The port was already under repeated attack from the Luftwaffe and much of the town was on fire and electricity and water supplies had been cut. Houses and cafés had been abandoned and food was scarce. Desperate times indeed.

A few hours after receiving the communication from the War Office to hold Calais to the last, the Germans were bearing down its outskirts. Gradually, the British were forced back towards the Old Town by the sheer weight of the German regiments from the 10th Panzer Division. The fighting was fierce in the ruined alleyways and in the bombed buildings, with the Riflemen disputing every street and defending every house. The British tanks proved to be no match for the German armour and against the well-armed German regiments the British infantry had only rifles, Bren Guns, the odd Lewis Gun and the ineffective Boys anti-tank rifle.

As they withdrew to the inner perimeter, the men took up defensive positions along the old walls and, as the battle progressed, Nicholson moved his headquarters into the old citadel. Nicholson ordered the King's Royal Rifles to hold the western sector of the walls and the Rifle Brigade the eastern walls. A contingent of the Queen Victoria Rifles, along with a number of French troops, occupied Fort Nieulay, the rest being held in reserve to reinforce the battalions manning the walls. ▶

ABOVE: The German advance sweeps on as a motorcycle and sidecar combination passes through the ruins of a French town during Hitler's offensive in the West. (Deutsches Bundesarchiv)

Nicholson made numerous requests for supplies, food, ammunition and support. But, in the end, all he received were messages.

'Defence of Calais to the utmost is of the highest importance to our country and our Army now', read one of the signals from Lord Gort. 'First, it occupies a large part of the enemy's armoured forces, and keeps them from attacking our line of communications. Secondly, it preserves a sally-port from which portions of the British Army may make their way home … The eyes of the Empire are upon you and the defence of Calais … His Majesty's government is confident that your gallant Regiments will perform an exploit worthy of the British name.'

Somehow, Nicholson's men hung on, and at 03.00 hours on 24 May, he received a signal from Major Dewing at the War Office: 'Evacuation [of the BEF] agreed in principle. When you have finished unloading vehicles, commence embarkation of all personnel except fighting personnel who will remain to cover final evacuation.' Nicholson was told that evacuation was 'probable' that night. When Churchill heard that

Nicholson had been told that he would be rescued, he was furious and sent an angry note to General Ismay: 'Vice-Chief of the Naval Staff informs me that [an] order was sent at 2 a.m. to Calais saying that evacuation was decided on in principle, but this is surely madness. The only effect of evacuating Calais would be to transfer the forces now blocking it to Dunkirk. Calais must be held for many reasons but especially to hold the enemy on its front.'

It was on this day – the 24th – that Hitler issued his famous instruction to General Guderian to halt his advance against the retreating British forces. The previous day, the commander of the Panzer Group, Generalfeldmarschall Paul von Kleist, reported that he had lost half of his tanks since the start of the campaign in the west. Accordingly, that evening Generaloberst von Rundstedt, in command of Army Group A, stopped his advance, and ordered him to simply blockade the Allied garrison in Calais. The Army High Command decided to give Army Group B the job of attacking the Allied pocket, while Army Group A would concentrate on guarding the southern flank of the German advance against a possible counterattack. Though Guderian had no choice but to comply with these orders in general terms, he pressed ahead with the attack upon Calais.

On the morning of the 25th, the 10th Panzers therefore renewed their attack, preceded by a heavy artillery bombardment. Every assault was repulsed but it was clear that 30 Brigade could not hold out much longer. So, in the afternoon, the German guns fell silent as General Schaal sent repeated demands into the town for Nicholson to surrender.

Nicholson would have none of it. 'If the Germans want Calais', Nicholson is reported to have said, 'they will have to fight for it'. But Nicholson had received a chilling message from Downing Street: 'Every hour you continue to exist is of the greatest help to the BEF. Government has therefore decided you must continue to fight. Have greatest possible admiration for your splendid stand. Evacuation will not (*repeat* not) take place and

craft required for the purpose are to return to Dover.'

Now they knew. The 30 Brigade was to be sacrificed.

By the next morning, the Rifle battalions could count only about 250 men each still under arms. After a lull in the fighting overnight, Schaal took up the battle once again with some 200 Junkers Ju 87 Stuka dive-bombers joining the attack. At around 11.00 hours the walls of the town were breached when one of the bastions was overrun. It was the end for 30 Brigade. Soon most of the town was in German hands and at 15.00 hours the citadel was taken.

Nicholson had no choice but to surrender. His men were marched away that evening to spend the next five years in captivity.

Just three hours after the fall of Calais the men of the BEF began embarking at Dunkirk.

The next day a signal was sent from Dover, from the Secretary of State to 'OC Troops Calais': 'Am filled with admiration for your magnificent fight which is worthy of the highest tradition of the British Army.'

The message was never received. ✠

ABOVE: **A British soldier pushes down the plunger to blow up a bridge (out of view) or similar structure in an attempt to impede the German advance in the Leuven region of Belgium, 1 June 1940.**

BELOW: **As the Blitzkrieg rolled relentlessly on, German troops soon found themselves on the battlefields of the First World War. The handwritten note on the rear of this image of a German anti-aircraft gun and a member of its crew, reveals that it was taken on 30 May 1940. In the background is Mount Kemmel which can be found some six miles south-west of Ypres.**

NOTES:
1. Alex Danchev and Daniel Todman, *War Diaries 1939-1945 Field Marshal Lord Alanbrooke* (Weidenfeld & Nicolson, London, 2001), p.59.
2. Winston S. Churchill, *The Second World War*, vol. II (Cassell, London, 1949), p.38.
3. Danchev and Todman, p.64.
4. J. Armengaud, *Le Drame de Dunkerque* (Plon, Paris, 1948), p.105.

DAY 1: 26 MAY

It was evident that the German penetration into northern France was unstoppable and that the Allies were heading for a catastrophic defeat. Unless the BEF could be evacuated back to the UK, it's army would be annihilated.

It was Sunday, 19 May 1940, when Vice-Admiral Bertram Ramsay, Flag Officer Commanding Dover, was summoned to the War Office in London for a meeting chaired by General Riddell-Webster, Quartermaster-General to the Forces. The subject they were to discuss, was 'the hazardous evacuation of very large forces' through Dunkirk, Calais and Boulogne. Ramsay was present because it was he who would be responsible for the evacuation and all available shipping would be placed at his disposal. It was envisaged that, starting on the 20th, the 'useless mouths', in other words the non-combatants, would be shipped back to the UK at the rate of 2,000 per day. Then, starting on the 22nd, the base personnel would be evacuated – some 15,000 in total. This would free the roads and the shipping for the vital third stage of the operation, to rescue the fighting divisions of the BEF.

ABOVE: **A head and shoulders portrait shot of Admiral Sir Bertram Ramsay who, on 24 August 1939, as a Vice-Admiral, was given command of the Dover area of operations – in which position he had responsibility for the Dunkirk evacuation. This photograph was taken at his London Headquarters in October 1943.**

Ramsay then called a meeting at Dover the following day. Ramsay's office at Dover was situated in the tunnels which had been excavated during the invasion threat from the French in the Napoleonic Wars. Though the tunnels had largely remained unoccupied since 1827, they were reopened following the outbreak of war in 1939. In the early months of the Second World War the tunnels were used as an air-raid shelter and then converted into an underground hospital.

The tunnels also became the Naval headquarters at Dover. The nerve centre of the headquarters was a single gallery which ended in an embrasure at the cliff face. This was where Ramsay had his office.

A succession of small rooms leading deep into the chalk away from Ramsay's office housed the Secretary, the Flag Lieutenant, the Chief of Staff (Captain L.V. Morgan) and the Staff office itself. Beyond these was a large room used normally for meetings/ conferences in connection with the operation of the Naval base. In the First World War, it

had held an auxiliary electrical plant and was known as the 'Dynamo Room'.

It was in that room, on 20 May, that Ramsay called his staff together to discuss the evacuation of the BEF. It was hoped that 10,000 men would be rescued every twenty-four hours from each of the three Continental ports – Dunkirk, Calais and Boulogne – with the thirty or so cross-Channel ferries, twelve steam-powered drifters and six coastal cargo ships that had been allocated to the task by the Admiralty. The ships would work the ports in pairs, with no more than two ships at any one time in the three harbours.

It was immediately obvious that a reorganisation of the base staff at Dover would be necessary to cope with the sudden rush of all the additional work. It was decided to set up this new body in the conference room itself. Thus, it was in this former Dynamo Room that the preparation, planning, and organisation of the evacuation of the British Expeditionary Force from France took place. It became known as Operation *Dynamo*. ▶

The location from where Operation *Dynamo* was organised and controlled. Situated on Castle Hill, Dover Castle is an English Heritage property which is described as 'the most iconic of all English fortresses commanding the gateway to the realm for nine centuries'.
(All images Historic Military Press unless stated otherwise)

One of the tunnels beneath Dover Castle which formed part of Vice-Admiral Bertram Ramsay's headquarters at the time of the evacuation. (© English Heritage)

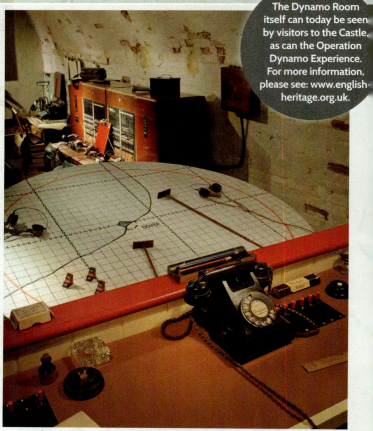

A view of one of the various rooms beneath Dover Castle, many of which had a part to play in Operation *Dynamo*. (© English Heritage)

The Dynamo Room itself can today be seen by visitors to the Castle, as can the Operation Dynamo Experience. For more information, please see: www.english-heritage.org.uk.

Ramsay's office was normally in Dover Castle, and the Dynamo room was hardly befitting a Royal Navy admiral, with a concrete floor partly covered by a thin strip of worn carpet, and a couple of charts to decorate its whitewashed walls. Its furniture consisted of a desk, and a few chairs around a conference table. The improvised nature of the new operations room reflected, in a manner, the nature of the great flotilla of vessels that would rescue the British Expeditionary Force.

The job of deciding exactly where the evacuation would take place from was handed to the BEF's acting Operations Officer, Lieutenant Colonel the Viscount Robert Bridgeman. Aware of the need for speed, Bridgeman set about his task immediately, and worked throughout the night. He started on the premise that an evacuation could take place anywhere between Calais and Ostend, he had to find a stretch of coast that could be easily reached by the retreating troops, and easily defended by the three corps of the BEF.

Bridgeman had, therefore, to consider which port had the best approach roads and which might offer some degree of protection from the air, and which ports had the best facilities. He had to answer such questions as, were there canals or other features which could be held against the enemy, particularly on the flanks, were there towns that could be held as strong-points and were

there dykes that could be opened to flood the ground and stop the German panzers?

After pouring over maps of the French and Belgium coasts, Bridgeman decided that the twenty-seven-mile stretch between Ostend and Dunkirk was the most suitable. By the morning of 22 May, Bridgeman had covered every detail he could think of. Each corps was allocated the routes it would use to reach the coast, and which stretch of coast each would hold. If the decision to evacuate was taken, there was now a plan in place.[1]

Ramsay attended a further meeting in London on that same day, Tuesday 22nd, to determine the number of vessels and small craft that could be employed in the rescue mission. Over the course of the following two days the evacuation of troops from Boulogne was started, and completed on 24 May. The evacuation at Calais was limited to lines of communications personnel, the fighting troops having

Vice-Admiral Bertram Ramsay briefs Winston Churchill in his underground headquarters, 28 August 1940.

to remain at the port to prevent German forces moving up from the south to cut off the BEF from the coast. This meant that if the BEF was to be evacuated, it could only be from Dunkirk and its adjacent coast.

In the few days since the first meeting in the War Office, the military situation had deteriorated so sharply that Ramsay was advised by the Admiralty on 26 May that Operation *Dynamo* was to be implemented immediately 'with the greatest vigour'. Ramsay was told that it was expected that the evacuation was likely to last for just two days before it would most likely be terminated by enemy action. He was advised that he would probably only be able to rescue 45,000 men.

EVACUATION

At around 10.30 hours on the morning of the 26th, Gort opened a telegram that had been sent from the Secretary of State for War, Oliver Stanley. It made chilling reading.

After informing Gort that the hoped-for French counter-offensive from the Somme would lack the strength to render any effective help to the armies fighting in the north, Stanley wrote, 'should this prove to be the case you will be faced with a situation in which the safety of the BEF will predominate. In such conditions [the] only course open to you may be to fight

Another of the rooms within the tunnel complex under Dover Castle, in this case the repeater station. (© English Heritage)

The entrance to Vice-Admiral Bertram Ramsay's subterranean headquarters at Dover Castle. (Courtesy of Robert Mitchell)

your way back to [the] West where all beaches and ports east of Gravelines will be used for embarkation. Navy will provide fleet of ships and small boats and RAF would give full support. As [the] withdrawal may have to begin very early, preliminary plans should be urgently prepared.'

Throughout the four terrible years of the First World War the BEF had dug in and held its ground. It was what the stubborn British Tommy did best. In this current conflict it was expected that the British Army would have to face another long slog on the Continent. Yet, after just two weeks, the British Government had already concluded that the situation in France was beyond redemption. Gort had been told to try and save the army, but with French resistance, and morale, collapsing, and the German panzer divisions speeding round the British flank, there seemed little prospect of the BEF being able to escape.

Gort replied solemnly that, 'I must not conceal from you that a great part of the BEF and its equipment will inevitably be lost even in the best circumstance'.

Lieutenant General Alan Brooke, who commanded II Corps, concurred with Gort's pessimistic assessment of the BEF's predicament: 'Nothing but a miracle can save the BEF now and the end cannot be far off,' he had written in his diary on 23 May. Three days later, after being briefed by Gort on the decision to evacuate, he calculated that, 'It is going to be a very hazardous enterprise and we shall be lucky if we save 25% of the BEF!'[2]

General Sir Edmund Ironside, Chief of the Imperial General Staff, expressed similar views: 'We shall have lost practically all our trained soldiers by the next few days – unless a miracle appears to help us.'

Britain, it seemed, was about to lose its army and was heading for a catastrophic defeat, unparalleled in its once-proud history.

THE DUNKIRK DEFENCES

Gort now had to plan the withdrawal, and by the evening of the 26th, he had drawn up his arrangements for the retreat to the coast in and around the port of Dunkirk. At this stage the front held by the BEF extended for some 128 miles, an area far too large to be defended by the resources available. This area had to be progressively shrunk.

In discussions with Général Blanchard, who that just been promoted to General Officer Commanding the French 1st Army, it was agreed that the front would be reduced by fifty-eight miles, this reduction to take

ABOVE: A fraction of the fixtures and fittings that can still be seen in the underground sections of Dover Castle.

place over the course of the following three days, ending on 29 May. 'The difficulties of execution were great,' wrote Ian Hay in the official Government publication of what was termed 'the Battle of Flanders', 'for the corridor of withdrawal was growing narrower … especially the south side, where the canal line had been forced at several points – and the troops were invariably getting into one another's way. The roads were few and narrow, and the French troops added to the difficulties of the situation by bringing into the area considerable quantities of horse-transport. Pitiful crowds of refugees added to the congestion and tragedy of the scene.'

Alan Brooke's diary, which he had considered destroying for fear that it would fall into the hands of the enemy if he was captured, reveals his anger at the situation the BEF found itself in. He was particularly annoyed at the lack of control by the local French authorities. The town of Armentières had been badly bombed and half the buildings in the town had been demolished, which included the mental institution and the inmates had been left to wander free: 'These lunatics let loose at that time were the last straw! With catastrophe on all sides, bombarded by rumours of every description, flooded by refugees and a demoralized French army, bombed from low altitude, and now on top of it all lunatics in brown corduroy suits standing at the side of the road grinning at one with an inane smile, a flow of saliva running from the corner of their mouths, and dripping noses![3] ▶

British troops making their way into Dunkirk as the evacuation gathers pace. According to the original caption, as 'the stream of soldiers and trucks must not be held up', a 'French marine fills in a crater caused by a German aerial bomb'.

After planning the withdrawal, Gort's next consideration was for a strong cordon, or bridgehead as Gort referred to it, around Dunkirk to protect the port as the troops were embarking. The task of establishing the bridgehead was handed to Lieutenant General Sir Ronald Adam. Gort asked the War Office if he could be sent a brigade of the 1st Canadian Division from the UK to provide him with a 'nucleus' of fresh and well-trained troops to help hold the bridgehead. At first this was agreed and orders were issued to ship the brigade to Dunkirk on the night of 26/7th, but then these orders were cancelled. It would be difficult enough to

rescue the troops already in France without adding to those numbers.

Adam immediately took command of all the troops in the Dunkirk area and began making arrangements to receive the 1st, 2nd and 3rd Corps and prepare lines of defence. He was told to 'act in conformity' with the French forces in the area, but only if this did not in any way endanger the British troops or impede their withdrawal. Dunkirk was under the direct orders of the Amiral du Nord, le contre-amiral Jean-Marie Charles Abrial, and subordinate to him was Général de Corps d'Armée Marie-Bertrand-Alfred Fagalde who was in command of the French XVI Corps.

ABOVE: **A street sign on the old D16 running into Dunkirk during or just after Operation *Dynamo*. Note the destroyed vehicle in the background.**

As the troops fell back, the lines of communication between the coast and the front line were being shortened by the hour. This meant that the rearward troops, who were no longer required, could be evacuated without delay, and with these men out of the way, the port could be left clear for the fighting troops – the ones who would have the enemy on their heels as they tried to escape.

Adam quickly set out his ideas for the defence of Dunkirk and the flat beaches to the north of the port. These beaches stretch to the Belgium border, eight miles away, and from there to Nieuport, nine and a half miles farther still. For the whole seventeen and a half miles the shore is a wide belt of shelving sand behind which are mile after mile of sand dunes, partially clothed in long, sharp spouts

A German despatch rider liaises with other troops amongst abandoned British and French vehicles and equipment near Dunkirk during Operation *Dynamo*.

of grass and patches of sea thistle. Set amid the dunes are the little resorts of Malo les Bains, Bray Dunes and La Panne. Away from the coast beyond the dunes was, in 1940, a wide strip of open land – common and meadow – leading to the Dunkirk to Furnes canal.

The French defences of Dunkirk were based on the peacetime organisation of the Secteur Fortifié des Flandres. These comprised inner and outer sectors, and to man these defences General Fagalde had a collection of local troops, equivalent to a weak division, plus the French 68th Division which had just withdrawn from Belgium. The local troops were deployed on the outer line and the 68th Division was handed the task of holding the French part of the inner sector.

A key part of the Dunkirk defensive scheme was the inundation of the ground to the west of the port as far as Bergues. Fagalde immediately put this in hand, opening the sluices on the River Aa. It was this western side of the perimeter that Fagalde and Gort agreed that the French should be responsible for, with the British being responsible for the eastern half which reached as far as Nieuport.

THE WITHDRAWAL TO THE DUNKIRK PERIMETER

The retreat was undertaken amid chaotic conditions, with abandoned vehicles and a flood of fleeing civilians blocking the roads.

ABOVE: **The statue of Admiral Sir Bertram Ramsay KCB, KBE, MVO, which was unveiled in the grounds of Dover Castle in November 2000.** (Paulina Grunwald/Shutterstock)

'The refugees continued to present a sorry picture indeed,' Lance Corporal Kenneth Carver, 5th Motor Ambulance Convoy RASC, later remembered. 'It was heart-rending to see the people with all their worldly belongings on their carts, shoulders, wheelbarrows, perambulators … You had to push these people aside while trying hard not to cause casualties, but invariably you pushed a cart or wheelbarrow into a hedge, and your instructions were to keep going and not to help people at all … These people were travelling for miles and miles with no food or water or accommodation.'[4]

The orders to retreat were also puzzling to the British troops who had, in many cases, not been heavily engaged, and certainly had not been beaten. Second Lieutenant Peter Martin was with the 2nd Battalion, Cheshire Regiment: 'We went from river to canal to river all the way back until we were told we were heading for Dunkirk and evacuation. As my battalion hadn't been troubled desperately by the Germans at all, it was incomprehensible.'

Some men, though, had to fight their way to the coast, and many became isolated from their parent units, struggling along in small groups, or joining others who seemed to know where they were going. Many men marched into the perimeter after marching all night on the packed roads. In the darkness, some had lost their officers and had just made their way along with others heading for the coast. This disorganisation was later commented on by the man who become the Senior Naval Officer at Dunkirk, but it must be remembered that the BEF had not trained its men for such a circumstance as the soldiers now found themselves in. It must also not be forgotten that few of the men had ever tried to get into a boat in three or four feet ▶

This black granite memorial at Teddington Lock commemorates the part played in Operation *Dynamo* by the Tough Brothers' boatyard. As preparations for the evacuations gathered pace, the boatyard's proprietor, Douglas Tough, received an early-morning telephone call from Admiral Sir Lionel Preston. Taking Tough into his confidence, Preston briefly outlined Operation *Dynamo*, the kind of boats needed and, most importantly, the urgency of the situation. The results were dramatic. Assisted by individuals such as Ron Lenthall and Chief Foreman Harry Day, Douglas Tough set about gathering the small craft asked for, starting with fourteen in his yard opposite Teddington Lock, a complex of three locks and a weir on the River Thames at Ham about a mile below Kingston-upon-Thames. 'More than 100 craft from the Upper Thames were [duly] assembled at the Ferry Road Yard of Tough Bros.,' notes an account by the Association of Dunkirk Little Ships. 'Here everything unnecessary was taken off and stored … The boats were then checked over and towed by Toughs and other tugs down river to Sheerness. Here they were fuelled and taken to Ramsgate where Naval Officers, Ratings and experienced volunteers were put aboard and directed to Dunkirk.' Interestingly, some scenes from the 1958 feature film *Dunkirk* were filmed around Teddington Lock. (Courtesy of Robert Mitchell)

A pre-war image of the ferry *Isle of Guernsey* which participated in the Dunkirk evacuation. Serving as a hospital ship, *Isle of Guernsey* made three trips across the Channel before she was pulled out of service due to an accumulation of damage from German air attacks.

of water, and certainly not after marching and fighting for days on end with little sleep or food.

But if the BEF had not planned or prepared for the situation it now found itself in, neither had the Germans. With no-one at the German High Command, the Oberkommando des Heeres (OKH), quite sure what to do, the enthusiastic statement by a Chief of the Luftwaffe General Staff General der Flieger Hans Jeschonnek that he could destroy the British from the air, was quickly seized upon. But the commanders of the Fliegerkorps, the air groups that would have to carry out the bombing, were less enthusiastic whilst there was a far bigger prize – the complete capture of France – in the offing. So, whilst the operations against the BEF were considerable, much of the Luftwaffe's effort towards the end of May was focussed elsewhere.

The Germans believed that the BEF was trapped and stood little chance of getting away. This was, in large measure, due to the calculations of Generaladmiral Schniewind, who told the chief of the Luftwaffe Göring on 26 May that, 'a regular and orderly transport of large numbers of troops with equipment cannot take place in the hurried and difficult conditions prevailing … Evacuation of troops without equipment, however, is conceivable

ABOVE: **The W-class destroyer HMS *Wolsey* pictured following her return from one of the crossings she made to Dunkirk under the command of Lieutenant Commander Colin Henry Campbell RN. Her first trip, as Campbell noted, had been four days before the official start of *Dynamo*: 'HMS *Wolsey* was ordered to proceed to Dunkirk at 19.13 22nd May. Ship berthed at the Felix Faure jetty and loaded about 200 wounded soldiers (all walking cases). Ship sailed for Dover at 21.05, secured to Admiralty Pier at 0140/23 and disembarked wounded, finally securing to buoy at 02.30.'**

by means of large numbers of smaller vessels, coastal and ferry steamers, fishing trawlers, drifters, and other small craft, in good weather, even from the open coast. The [Royal] Navy, however, is not in a position to take part successfully in this with the means at its disposal. There are no signs yet of such transport being carried out or prepared.'

How wrong he was.

DAY 1

Operation *Dynamo* was set to commence at 18.57 hours on the evening of 26 May 1940. One of the first tasks that had to be undertaken was that of establishing a secure route across the Channel. There was little point in rescuing the soldiers from the panzers for them to be sunk by the U-boats or the Stukas. So, Ramsay had to

form a protective screen to the eastwards of the evacuation area and provide anti-aircraft defences. Ramsay also sent his minesweepers to clear the seas around Dunkirk. The defence of Dunkirk port and its beaches would be the responsibility of Fighter Command. Now, though, came Ramsay's greatest task – that of finding enough vessels to rescue the BEF.

On the 26th, the only vessels immediately available were fifteen personnel ships, which were mainly cross-Channel or Irish Sea ferries, or packets, which were at Dover or in the Downs, with a further seventeen at Southampton. Also at Southampton were three Dutch and Belgian ferries. There were six coastal ships and sixteen wooden and steel barges in the Downs. Thirty-nine or forty Dutch coasters, or skoots, had escaped across the North Sea to British ports and were available as well as thirty-two motor transport ships, stores ships and tankers.[5]

ABOVE: **A view of the Armed Boarding Vessel *King Orry* as she appeared during her First World War service.** (Courtesy of Harvey Milligan)

BELOW: **Pictured here in her civilian role with the Isle of Man Steam Packet Company, the steamer *Mona's Isle* was the first ship to complete a round trip during Operation *Dynamo*. Having sailed from Dover at 21.16 hours on 26 May, she returned fifteen hours later, despite being shelled and attacked by aircraft (which left twenty-three dead and sixty wounded), to disembark over 1,400 soldiers.** (Courtesy of Harvey Milligan)

Except for the destroyer HMS *Wolsey*, which left Dover at 19.30 hours, the steamer *Mona's Isle* was the first ship to sail on the great mission to rescue the BEF. On the outbreak of war *Mona's Isle*, which used to operate passenger services between the Isle of Man and Belfast and Dublin, had been requisitioned by the Admiralty and fitted out as an Armed Boarding Vessel. She reached Dunkirk around midnight, berthing at the Quai Félix Faure as the Luftwaffe was bombing the harbour. *Mona's Isle* took off 1,420 men and, upon reaching Dover, became the first ship of Operation *Dynamo* to make the return trip.[6]

Another of those personnel ships that arrived at Dunkirk on that first day of the evacuation was the Southern Railway Company's *Maid of Orleans*. Serving as Chief Engineer on the ferry was George Frederick Tooley: 'The harbour and port made a depressing sight. Burning oil tanks and dense clouds of smoke spread a pall of gloom, which to some extent prevented exact detection by hostile aircraft and gave some cover to those sorely in need of it. A considerable number of wrecks in the vicinity and approaches made navigation a nightmare. All this came as a profound shock to those of us who had previously been

The view of the Port of Dover as seen from the wartime gun emplacements at St Martin's Battery on the town's Western Heights. On the right is the Admiralty Pier, where most of the men brought back to Dover were disembarked, though the port's Eastern Arm and Prince of Wales Pier were also employed.

A survivor of the first day of Operation *Dynamo*. On display at the Imperial War Museum, Duxford, Supermarine Spitfire Mk.Ia N3200 is an ex-19 Squadron aircraft which is seen here in the QV squadron codes it wore when it was shot down on 26 May 1940. Squadron Leader Geoffrey Stevenson, the CO of 19 Squadron, was the pilot at the time. The squadron had been detailed to patrol the Dunkirk area when, following a raid by a force of Junkers Ju 87s on the port, it was attacked by a group of Messerschmitt Bf 109s from 1./JG1 and 2./JG2. In the subsequent melee, N3200 was hit in the radiator, forcing Stevenson to make a belly-landing on the beach at Sangatte. The remains of N3200 were excavated in 1986 and spent a few years on display in a French museum before returning to the UK in 2000, at which point the restoration to flying condition began.
(Courtesy of Robert Mitchell)

engaged in trooping from Southampton to Cherbourg in orderly convoys with no more excitement than an occasional U-boat or E-boat scare or a German plane reconnaissance.[7]

The hospital carriers *Isle of Guernsey* and *Worthing* left Dover at midday and came under aerial attack when off Calais. Nevertheless, they both reached Dunkirk that night, their passage into the harbour being illuminated by the fires that raged along the docks and across the town. They each embarked about 300 stretcher cases and made their way back to England under the cover of darkness.

The Armed Boarding Vessel SS *King Orry*, a former Isle of Man Steam Packet Company passenger ship, managed to sail into Dunkirk harbour where she embarked 1,131 soldiers. Commander J. Elliot RNR cast off and in the early hours of 27 May, *King Orry* reached Dover. She ran the gauntlet of fire from the batteries as she passed Calais, being hit, resulting in a number of casualties on board. Nevertheless, the steamer reached Dover, docking just before midday.

The only small boats available that could get close in to take men directly off the beaches were the cutters and whalers, i.e. the rowing boats carried by Royal Navy ships. This meant that most of the troops would have to be collected from the harbour itself. But Dunkirk was a forbidding place, of which the historian David Divine, writing in the 1950s, painted a graphic, if grim, picture, portraying the last hours of the first day of the evacuation:

'The port of Dunkirk as darkness fell this Sunday was a place of horror. To the west of the great basin enclosed by the outer moles the oil-tank farm was blazing. Flames silhouetted the moles and lit the underside of the bascule bridge that was jammed open at the entrance to the main basin, and the high, white column of the lighthouse. Warehouses up and down the 115 acres of the basin were burning. The wrecked cranes were outlined against their brilliance. Smoke lifted intermittently to show the fires of the town itself. And endlessly through the night the thunder of the bombs and the lightning flash of their explosions marked the progress of destruction.'[8]

On this first day only 7,669 men had been evacuated, all of whom arrived in Britain on the 27th. It must have appeared that the Admiralty's estimate of only being able to rescue 45,000 men was probably reasonably accurate. There is no doubt that as day broke on 27 May, it appeared that the British Army was soon to experience a disaster on monumental scale. ✠

NOTES:
1. Walter Lord, *The Miracle of Dunkirk* (Allen Lane, London, 1982), p.20.
2. Danchev and Todman, pp.67 and 70.
3. ibid, p.69.
4. Quoted in Joshua Levine, *Forgotten Voices of Dunkirk* (Edbury Press, 2010), p.172.
5. David Divine, *The Nine Days of Dunkirk* (Ballantine Books, New York, 1959), pp.82–3.
6. W.J.R. Gardner, *The Evacuation from Dunkirk, 'Operation Dynamo 26 May–4June 1940* (Frank Cass, London, 2000), p.16.
7. David J. Knowles, *Escape from Catastrophe, 1940 Dunkirk* (self-published, Rochester, 2000), pp.77–8.
8. Divine, p.85.

SUBSCRIBE
TO *YOUR* FAVOURITE MAGAZINE
AND SAVE

DUNKIRK Special

EXCLUSIVES: DUNKIRK FILM & FALKLANDS CONTENT

A HISTORY OF CONFLICT

BRITAIN AT WAR ®

BRITAIN'S BEST SELLING MILITARY HISTORY MONTHLY

WIN!
20 x Signed Copies
of Dunkirk Film
Book to be won!
Closing Date: 8 September 2017

EXCLUSIVE
- Inside Story Of New Film
- The RAF At Dunkirk
- Admiral Ramsay's 'Dynamo' Miracle

DUNKIRK

www.britainatwar.com

VC HEROISM AT ALAMEIN
Victory And Bravery From
The Wreckage Of Defeat

FALKLANDS WAR OBSERVER'S ACCOUNT
Previously Untold Story Plus Unseen
Photographs

JULY 2017 ISSUE 123
UK £4.70

Britain at War is dedicated to exploring every aspect of Britain's involvement in conflicts from the turn of the 20th century through to modern day. From World War I to the Falklands, World War II to Iraq, readers are able to re-live decisive moments in Britain's history through fascinating insight combined with rare and previously unseen photography.

www.britainatwar.com

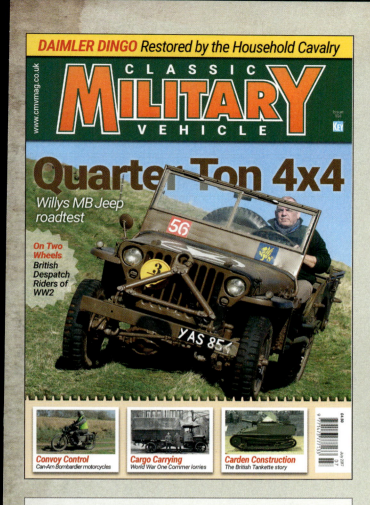

Though the British were in the throes of abandoning France, the French, in the form of Général Georges Blanchard, continued to cooperate with the fleeing Allies, agreeing to leave specified roads for the BEF's sole use. The roads, though, were narrow and badly congested with refugees.

The exact situation at Dunkirk, however, was unclear, so Captain William Tennant, chief staff officer to the First Sea Lord, volunteered to cross the Channel on the afternoon of 27 May and report his findings back to the Admiralty. With a naval beach and pier party of twelve officers and 160 ratings, plus communication staff, Tennant left Dover on HMS *Wolfhound* at 13.45 hours. On the way to France the destroyer was attacked by the Luftwaffe every thirty minutes between 16.00 hours and 18.00 hours.

One of these attacks was carried out by a group of four Ju 87s, two bombs hitting the water close to *Wolfhound*'s starboard bow. 'Splinters came on board,' reported Lieutenant Commander J.W. McCoy, 'the remaining salvoes were not close. *Wolfhound* opened fire and it is considered that two aircraft were hit. One aircraft emitting heavy smoke and another jettisoning its bombs about two miles away.'

It was at about 18.00 hours that *Wolfhound* pulled into Dunkirk, just as the port was under attack from a larger force of Stukas. The author Robert Jackson described the scene faced by Tennant and his team in his book *Dunkirk: The British Evacuation, 1940*: 'As *Wolfhound* approached Dunkirk … the pall of smoke assumed frightening proportions as it coiled and billowed in the summer air, and at its foot the whole waterfront seemed to be ablaze. Rivers of flame seethe along the quay from lines of burning warehouses, and as the destroyer approached the harbour a carpet of soot descended on her like black rain. The *Wolfhound* berthed to the screech and crump of bombs.'

BELOW: **British troops entering Dunkirk pass the smouldering wreckage of a lorry, a small part of the debris of war that increasingly came to litter the streets of the port.** (All images Historic Military Press unless stated otherwise)

With the town and port enveloped in dense smoke from the burning oil depots and refineries, Tennant disembarked his party, divided them up into sections and told the officers in charge of each section to 'scatter' their men around the port to make them less vulnerable to bombing attacks, whilst he made his way to the Naval Headquarters in Bastion 32. 'The sight of Dunkirk and nearby districts gave one a hollow feeling in the pit of the stomach,' wrote Tennant. 'The Boche had been going for it really hard, and there was not a pane of glass left anywhere – most of it was still lying in the streets. There were also "unremoved" dead lying about from the last air raid.'[1]

Tennant immediately realised that the port was untenable and that he could not maintain *Wolfhound* in Dunkirk to act as a radio link with Dover as he had hoped. *Wolfhound*, along with her sister ship *Wolsey*, was ordered to pick up some of the waiting troops and return to Dover. Tennant assumed the position of Senior Naval Officer, meeting with senior Army officers to discuss the situation in Dunkirk. The town had been heavily bombed; fires raged through the streets and, as Private William Ridley, 9th Battalion, Durham Light Infantry, graphically described, Dunkirk 'had the stink of death. It was the stink of blood and cordite.' ▶

DAY 2: 27 MAY

On the first full day of Operation *Dynamo* it was evident that the rate at which the troops were being evacuated was far too slow. The call went out for more ships – big and small.

BELOW: In 1940, Dunkirk still possessed a series of old fortifications that provided both seaward and landward defence. The most powerful of all these fortifications, known as *Bastion 32*, was used as a naval headquarters for the northern region of France. Situated on what was towards the head of the western side of the main channel of the harbour, it sits today by the Rue des Chantiers de France. Built in 1874, its thick walls housed the command post of the French naval officer in charge of Dunkirk, Amiral du Nord, le contre-amiral Jean-Marie Charles Abrial. It was in Bastion 32 that Tennant met Allied army and navy officers to discuss the evacuation.

Within two hours Tennant had made his assessment and he sent the following signal to Dover: 'Please send every available craft to beaches East of Dunkirk immediately. Evacuation tomorrow night is problematical.'[2]

Tennant needed every available craft because it was not possible for large ships alone to bring off the British troops. The port of Dunkirk had been largely destroyed by the Luftwaffe and concrete block-ships had been sunk at the harbour entrance. This left little for the ships to berth alongside apart from a wooden breakwater. This, the East Mole, was only five feet wide and had not been designed for embarking personnel. Apart from the Mole there were just the soft, sandy beaches, stretching for sixteen miles eastwards from Dunkirk to Nieuport. Ships could not approach the beaches, but small boats could. The boats could be used to ferry the troops from the beaches to the ships waiting off shore. So Tennant needed *every* available craft.

Because of the Small Craft Registration Order, the Admiralty held full details of all the boats that might be available within

a reasonable sailing distance of Dover. This order had gone out on 14 May, being broadcast by the BBC in the nine o'clock news. Its timing was quite coincidental, being a step taken by the Admiralty because of the increasing demand for vessels due to the general war situation, and was not a direct consequence of the Dunkirk evacuation. The order read as follows: 'The Admiralty have made an order requesting all owners of self-propelled pleasure craft between 30 and 100 feet in length, to send all particulars to the Admiralty within fourteen days from today, if they have not already offered or requisitioned.'

Soon all the owners or operators of tugs, ferries, barges, motor-launches, lighters, fishing boats and schooners, as well as boat-yards, boat-builders and yacht clubs up and down the Thames and along the south and south-eastern coasts, were being contacted by the Ministry of Shipping. Early on the morning of the 27th, the Admiralty had already asked the Ministry of Sea Transport to find between forty and fifty such small craft to assemble at

Sheerness for 'a special requirement'. The Director of the Small Vessels Pool, Vice-Admiral Sir Lionel Preston, provided a list of those vessels from the Small Craft Register that he thought would be able to assist with the evacuation, but it was soon found that many were not suitable.

A meeting was hurriedly arranged with the Director of Sea Transport, H.C. Riggs, in which it was agreed that Vice-Admiral Preston would despatch some of his officers to examine the boat-yards from Teddington, on the Thames, to Burnham and Brightlingsea on the coast, and to send all vessels that they thought fit for service round to Sheerness. Until these vessels could be collected and organised, there remained very few small boats available to take men off the beaches.

ABOVE: A French Army Renault UE Chenillette light tracked armoured carrier is pictured having been abandoned in one of Dunkirk's side streets.

LEFT: The kind of scene that greeted Tennant upon his arrival at Dunkirk. The original caption states that this is the 'first picture of the destruction of Dunkirk ... a square in the centre of Dunkirk photographed during the incessant Nazi bombardment of the French port. The smoke and dust of battle hangs over everything, while in the background is seen a wall falling from a partially demolished building. In the centre of the square the statue of Jean Bart, the famous French corsair, seems to be threatening the invader with his sword.'

According to the French censor-approved caption on the rear of this wartime image, it shows civilians making their way to safety during the German bombardment of Dunkirk.

BELOW: **A view of the W-class destroyer HMS *Worcester*. On 24 May 1940, *Worcester* was assigned to Operation *Dynamo*. She made six trips to the Dunkirk beaches, transporting a total of 4,350 Allied troops to the UK. She was damaged in a German air raid on 27 May 1940.**

The main effort of the 27th, therefore, was focussed on pressing the ferries to undertake as many trips to Dunkirk as possible. This was maintained at a rate of two every three and a half hours throughout the day, but this came at a heavy cost. Between sailings timed 03.00 hours and 15.00 hours, no less than five transports were shelled and returned to the UK without making the trip, and another, *Mona's Isle*, was damaged by shell fire.

Returning by what was designated Route Z, which took the Isle of Man Steam Packet Company vessel southwards passed Gravelines and Cap Gris Nez before heading out for Dover, *Mona's Isle* came under fire from German batteries on the beach and from coastal batteries taken over by the invaders. Shells fell all around, sending plumes of water high into the air and at least two hit the boat. *Mona's Isle* was then attacked by approximately eight Messerschmitt Bf 109s. On board *Mona's Isle* was Denys Thorp RNVR, who later reached the rank of Lieutenant Commander:

'Four or five ratings were wounded. Petty Officer Pope RNR though badly wounded in the wrist closed some ready use lockers in the 12-pounder enclosure after the 12-pounder crew were knocked out, in the face of heavy machine-gun and cannon fire and afterwards received the DSC. The plight of the soldiers wounded was more tragic as after what they had endured in France they came aboard this ship thankful to be in the Navy's care and bound for home with the feeling that their troubles were for the moment at an end. I was very upset by this aspect at the time and it took me a long time to forget that no doctor was carried and no sick bay attendant, but their mates came to their help and did what they could for them.

'The ship was in a sorry state and when the damage was assessed the situation did not look too bright. It was found that the tele-motor pipes were severed and the ship could not be steered as the hand steering gear had been removed when the ship was converted. All the boats were shot up and rendered useless and the wireless aerial had been carried away, the W/T set out of action. Many steam pipes were leaking and steam and hot water were issuing from unexpected places.'[3]

Luckily, the white cliffs of Dover were in sight, and so by careful use of port and starboard engines, the packet was able to reach the safety of the port. Twenty-three men on board had been killed and a further sixty wounded. It was the last effort by the packet steamer, which, in her two trips, had taken 2,634 men from Dunkirk.

The cargo ship MV *Sequacity* did not even reach Dunkirk. Her loss was reported by her skipper Captain J. MacDonald:

'All went well until we arrived off Calais, then I noticed some shells falling in the water ahead of us. I thought it was land batteries ashore firing at some mines, but soon after the shells started dropping all around my ship, and one came through the port side, at the water line in the main hold and went out the starboard side.

'I sent my mate down into the hold with some of the crew to try and patch the hole up. The next shot came through the port side of the engine room and smashed up the auxiliary engines that drove our dynamo, etc., put our switchboard out of action, and went out the starboard side. This put our pumps entirely out of action for pumping water out of the hold. ▶

BELOW: **Troops line the Mole at Dunkirk during Operation *Dynamo* as Royal Navy personnel look on from a ship tied up alongside.**

BELOW: **There can be little doubt that the forty or so Dutch skoots (or schuits) which participated in Operation *Dynamo* played an invaluable part in its success. These vessels were a self-propelled seagoing development of the towed barges so familiar on European rivers such as the Rhine, Elbe and Danube. Close examination of this image suggests that it depicts the skoot *Hilda* en route to Dunkirk towing a collection of smaller boats. *Hilda* had been lying at Poole when she was taken over by a crew commanded by Lieutenant A. Gray RN. During her three trips she transported 835 men.**

'Another shot came through the wheelhouse and went through the hatches, down the forehold, and right through the ship's bottom.'[4]

If this was not bad enough, the Luftwaffe then appeared overhead, and its bombers attacked both *Sequacity* and the accompanying collier *Yewdale*. More shells rained in on the stricken coaster and to make matters even worse the wind increased, causing a 'nasty' swell which caused water to lap into the hole in *Sequacity*'s side. The coaster began to list. *Sequacity* was clearly going down, and rapidly.

Captain MacDonald blew on the ship's horn to attract *Yewdale*'s attention, but amid the noise and confusion of battle this was not noticed. An RAF fighter happened to be flying over the two ships and saw that *Sequacity* was in trouble. The aircraft dropped red flares ahead of *Yewdale* and the crew on board the collier looked back to see *Sequacity* stationary in the water and listing severely. MacDonald launched *Sequacity*'s lifeboat and his crew made it safely to *Yewdale* as the coaster went down by the head.

As a result of the damage inflicted on *Mona's Isle*, and with the loss of *Sequacity*, Ramsay reported to the Admiralty that the normal channel, Dover to Dunkirk, was impracticable in daylight owing to fire from shore batteries extending from Les Hemmes to Gravelines. This meant using the route through the Zuydecoote Pass to the north of Dunkirk, which extended the distance of the round trip from eighty miles to 172 resulting in a general slowing up of traffic. This route had to be swept before it could be used. Work was also commenced to sweep a channel from the North Goodwin to the Ruytingen Pass and thence into the Dunkirk Roads, thus shortening the round trip from 172 miles to 108.

To help speed up the turn-round rate of the ships, five UK ports were to be used to disembark the troops. The destroyers were to use Dover; drifters, skoots, coasters and minesweepers were to sail into Margate or Ramsgate as directed; the personnel ships were to go to Folkestone; and, lastly, the cruiser *Calcutta* was to disembark at Sheerness.

In the afternoon four steam packets – *Queen of the Channel*, *St Seiriol*, *Maid of Orleans*, *Isle of Thanet* and two hospital ships left Dover at 13.30 hours. Of these, *Queen of the Channel* and *St Seiriol* arrived in Dunkirk harbour at around 19.30 hours in the middle of an air raid. *Queen of the Channel*, a ferry and tourist packet which in peacetime had operated under her skipper, Captain O'Dell, along the English east coast and across the Channel to French, Belgian and Dutch ports, had barely started embarking troops when she was ordered to leave the harbour and make her way to the beaches to the east. Using her own boats she lifted about 150 men from the beaches before being ordered back to the harbour, where she collected a further 700 men. In the early hours of the 28th *Queen of the Channel* set off for the UK.

The scene on the quayside in Dunkirk after a Luftwaffe air raid.

BELOW: **One of the many vessels that participated in the Dunkirk evacuation, the Training Ship *St Seiriol*.**

German troops pick their way through possessions and equipment (including various vehicles) abandoned by soldier and civilian alike on the roads leading to Dunkirk.

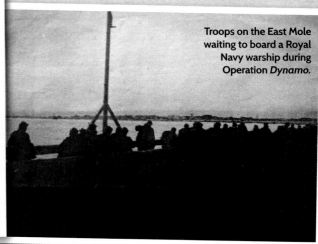

Troops on the East Mole waiting to board a Royal Navy warship during Operation *Dynamo*.

Meanwhile, when *St Seiriol* arrived at Dunkirk she tied up on the East Mole to await instructions. This Liverpool and North Wales Steamship Company ship normally operated between Liverpool and Llandudno around Anglesey. She also undertook trips to Douglas, Isle of Man. Her Chief Engineer was J. McNamee:

'There was an air raid in progress as we arrived alongside. Our guns with others were in action. We landed a man on the pier [Mole] to hang on to our ropes. About 8 p.m. Lieutenant Commander Williams, R.N., came on board and told the captain to proceed out of the harbour, lower his boats, and get the men on board from the beach.

'We got to the anchorage. I lowered the first boat in charge of the second officer and the second boat in charge of R. Thomas, A.B. The third boat was taken by the crew of a trawler.

'When I was about to lower the fourth boat we received information that there were a number of troops arriving at the pier. With the remainder of the crew we still had on board we proceeded alongside the pier We got about 600 men on board, they were arriving in batches, about 11 p.m. we were told that there were no more men in the vicinity, so we cut our mooring ropes. On hearing more men running along the pier we got the ship alongside the pier again and got about 80 more on board.'

During its stay by the Mole, the harbour was bombed in four separate raids, and as *St Seiriol* was moving off from the Mole, the German aircraft dropped illuminated

parachute flares which lit up the whole scene. The ferry then went back towards La Panne to pick up the boats he had dropped off, but was ordered to make his way to Dover via Calais.

The passenger vessel *Canterbury*, entered Dunkirk harbour at 22.00 hours, and left 58 minutes later having been loaded with 457 troops, including 140 stretcher cases.

Isle of Thanet, formerly a cross-Channel ferry for Southern Railways serving the Folkestone to Boulogne route and then the Southampton St Malo service, was commissioned as Hospital Carrier No. 22 on 5 September – just two days after the declaration of war – and was based at Newhaven. One of her engineers was Brian Murray:

ABOVE: **This plaque hung in the saloon entrance of** *St Seiriol* **and is inscribed with a message of thanks received from the Minister of Shipping expressing admiration of courage and endurance of Master and his crew during** *Dynamo*.

'I stood on the deck of our fast-moving ship wondering why we were heading east into the rising sun and not as usual south towards Dieppe. We arrived into Dunkirk about lunchtime. All was quiet, extremely quiet. The quayside was deserted, so unlike what we would expect to see. A British destroyer followed us in and moored up alongside. I remember the lettering on her bows. It was L.20.[5]

'Within half an hour the war really began – the banging and shooting war that was to go on for five long years. Several German planes arrived and as they proceeded to drop bombs, our friends in the destroyer opened up and engaged them with her 4in. guns to the detriment of the chief steward's crockery and my nerves. As you can imagine, that complacency of ours that had taken seven long months to develop was dispelled in almost one bang – I know that mine was.

'During that small battle between our navy and the Luftwaffe a hospital train ran on to the dockside and immediately the ship came to life. All the ship's company not on duty turned to and assisted the hospital staff, which consisted of some 40 men and officers with 6 Queen Alexandra's Army Nursing Service sisters, to load on the wounded. Later that evening, having experienced almost continuous hostile air attack during our stay, we got underway and steamed for Newhaven.'

Such was the aerial bombardment endured by Dunkirk on the 27th, the Luftwaffe mounted 225 conventional bomber and seventy-five dive-bomber attacks on the port, ▶

BELOW: **A pre-war image of the paddle steamer** *Brighton Belle*. **During a crossing on the evening of 27 May 1940, this vessel brought back some 800 troops, but hit a submerged wreck forcing the paddle steamer** *Medway Queen* **to come to its aid.**

ABOVE: This information panel relating to the East Mole can be seen at the base of the harbour's eastern arm, off which the jetty stretched out to sea at the time of the evacuation.

RIGHT: Troops on the East Mole boarding a Royal Navy warship. The poor quality of this image is due to the fact that it is an example of a 'Wirephoto', when images were sent, in this case to the US for immediate publication, by telegraph or telephone.

dropping more than 350 tons of ordnance. The first of these raids, delivered by the Heinkel He 111s of KG 1 and KG 4, struck the harbour, destroying seven docking basins, five miles of quays and 115 acres of docks and warehouses. The second wave that morning, from KG 54, hit and sank the French steamer *Aden* near the eastern Mole.

This was followed by an attack by Ju 87s, the bombs dropped sinking the French steamer *Côte d'Azur* and an auxiliary mine-sweeper. The Stukas also sank the small British coaster, *Worthtown*. The last raid was by Dornier Do 17Zs of KG 2 and KG 3, which wrecked the railway yards and struck the Saint-Pol refinery.

The RAF did respond, mounting 287 sorties along the coast from Gravelines as far as Ostend, claiming to have shot down twenty-one German bombers, with the loss of fourteen Hurricanes and five Spitfires.[6] Fighter Command's aircraft had, of course, limited time over the French and Belgian coasts, and it was not possible to predict when the next German raid was to be delivered. This meant that often the Luftwaffe could fly unimpeded over Dunkirk and the adjacent beaches, leading to many complaints from the soldiers that they had been abandoned by the RAF. It was not true.

At 20.25 hours Ramsay received a 'Most Immediate' message from Captain Tennant, which read: 'Port consistently bombed all day, and on fire. Embarkation possible only from beaches East of harbour A.B.C.D. Send all ships and passenger ships there to anchor.'

What Tennant was referring to was that the beach east of Dunkirk, from Malo les Bains through Bray Dunes to La Panne, had been divided to four zones – A, B, C, and D respectively. So Tennant then sent parties along the shore to La Panne to organise the beaches to allow for the orderly passage of the troops through the beaches onto the boats. All the ships that subsequently reached Dunkirk were ordered to the beaches.

The Dutch skoots *Lena*, *Hebe II*, and *Oranje* also reached France on the 27th, and anchored off the beaches and embarked troops during the night, setting off on their return trips in the early hours of the 28th.

Some of the others (*Bernrif*, *Brandaris*, *Hondsrug*, *Jutland*, *Patria*, *Tilly* and *Twente*) were within sight of Dunkirk when, due to a miscommunication, they returned to the Downs. What actually happened was that the signal was sent to 'turn back ships attempting to enter Dunkirk'. This was meant to mean that the ships should go instead to the beaches. Understandably, this was interpreted as meaning that the ships should return to the UK.

THE LAST CHANCE

The situation was grave, with the French army in a state of near anarchy. The situation was equally perilous at Dunkirk, which was under almost continual bombardment, and every cellar or possible bomb-proof shelter was crammed with soldiers. With the passage

The East Mole at Dunkirk, as it was in 1940, no longer exists, though this is the spot from where it reached out into the harbour. The East Mole was not a stout stone wall with berthing places along its length, as might be imagined around a harbour. It was a narrow plank-way barely wide enough for three men to walk abreast. On either side was a protective railing made of strong timbers with, at intervals, taller posts which could be used by ships to secure themselves against the Mole in emergencies. At the far end of the Mole was a concrete 'nose' upon which stood a short lighthouse. The Mole was built in this fashion to allow the tides to roll in and out and to put less strain upon its structure.

LEFT: **Loaded with evacuated soldiers, *Emperor of India* sets out from Dunkirk to return to the South Coast ports during Operation *Dynamo*.**

A pre-war image of the paddle steamer *Emperor of India*, which made at least one crossing to Dunkirk, this being recorded as having occurred on the evening of 27 May 1940.

of every hour increasing numbers of men filed into the town, many having lost touch with their parent units, and, wandering through the rubble-strewn streets, they were inviting targets for the Luftwaffe.

The harbour itself was an even easier target for the German bombers, and stationary ships berthed there were in deadly danger. Dunkirk had become too dangerous for the Royal Navy, but with the few small boats that were available, embarkation from the beaches was painfully slow. Tennant saw only one solution to the problem – to use the Moles, or breakwaters, that protected the harbour to the east and west. These stone, concrete and wooden arms were long and narrow (only five feet wide) and were not designed for embarking people. But ships could berth alongside them without the risk of being trapped inside the harbour, where they were

ABOVE: **The bust of Admiral Sir William Tennant located in the grounds of the Bell Tower (often referred to as the 'Pepperpot' by virtue of its distinctive appearance), which dominates Church Street in Upton-upon-Severn, Worcestershire. It is said that without Tennant's cool head and organisational skills, Operation *Dynamo* would not have achieved the results that it did. He came to be known by the nickname 'Dunkirk Joe'.** (With the kind permission of Nick Oliver)

also easy targets. The East Mole, in particular, stretched for nearly a mile out to sea and could accommodate many ships at a time.

The priority back in the UK, however, was to despatch as many small vessels as possible to help lift the troops from the beaches. The Naval Officer in Charge, Ramsgate, had the job of arranging the fuelling and despatching of all small power boats and the larger boats that would tow the smaller vessels across the Channel. Rear Admiral A.H. Taylor became 'Dynamo Maintenance Officer' at Sheerness, tasked with making sure the boats, particularly the towing vessels, were in a suitable condition for the stresses they would be under on the long trip to Dunkirk.

Once out at sea, it was not possible to contact these boats by radio and during the crossing some became detached from their tows. Much time was lost trying to gather up the lost boats.

Over in Dunkirk, Tennant was unimpressed with the chaotic state of the army as the first troops gathered on the beaches: 'As regards the behaviour and bearing of the troops, both British and French, prior to and during the embarkation, it must be recorded that the earlier parties were embarked off the beaches in a condition of completed disorganisation. There appeared to be no military officers in charge of the troops, and the impression was undoubtedly enhanced by the difficulty in distinguishing between the uniforms of such officers as were present and those of other ranks. It was soon realised that it was vitally necessary to dispatch naval officers in their unmistakable uniforms, with armed beach parties to take charge of the soldiers on shore immediately prior to embarkation.'[7] Before the arrival of these naval officers, Tennant's party was sent to the beaches to 'police' the troops and keep some kind of order, where each of the three Corps of the BEF had been allocated a section of beach.

Only two of the personnel ships actually made the round trip during the 27th. The first of these was the General Steam Navigation Company's MV *Royal Daffodil*, which

normally took passengers from London to Ostend. It left Dover at 10.54 hours under escort of the destroyer *Vimy*. They formed a convoy with HMS *Anthony*, which was escorting the SS *Kyno*, though these latter two were called back in mid-Channel. *Anthony* and *Royal Daffodil* were then joined by the hospital ships *St Andrew* and *St Julien*. *Royal Daffodil* succeeded in recovering 840 men and headed back to the UK.

The second to make the round trip on the 27th, was the Great Western Railway Steamer *St Helier* which was ordered back before she could embark any troops. *Wolfhound* and *Wolsey* recovered 206 and 130 respectively from the beach at Malo, but these destroyers did not depart for Dover until after midnight.[8]

In addition, seventeen drifters of the Dover Command sailed from Dover for the beach at Malo-les-Bains, and during the night lifted 2,000 troops from the beach by ships' dinghies. With more than 200,000 men waiting on the beaches, or fighting their way through to Dunkirk, the number of troops rescued was alarmingly small.

It was disappointing to all concerned that after two days so few men had been rescued. There was not much time left to save the BEF, and the continuing success of the entire operation depended on how long the Germans could be kept at bay. On the night of 26/27 May, the 1st and 2nd Corps had swung back with their right resting on Fort de Sainghin to the south-east of Lille. The Navy would get at least one more day to try and save the army.

NOTES:
1. Quoted in Knowles, p.44.
2. D. Divine, p.95.
3. Thorp's story can be found at: www.website.lineone.net/-tom_lee/monas%20isle%20hms.htm.
4. Divine, pp.93–4.
5. Pennant No. L.20 was allocated to the Hunt-class destroyer HMS *Garth*.
6. Douglas C. Dildy, *Dunkirk 1940, Operation Dynamo* (Osprey, Oxford, 2010), p.36.
7. Tennant's report can be found in TNA ADM 199/789.
8. Gardner, p.25.

DAY 3: 28 MAY

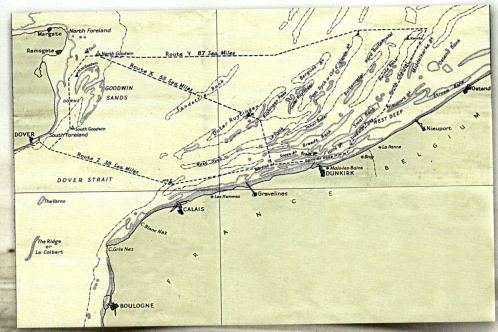

The evacuation from Dunkirk was proving painfully slow, but at last, the 'Little Ships' entered the fray.

LEFT: A plan showing the routes, together with their distances, which were used between Dover and Dunkirk during Operation *Dynamo*.

Apart from the East Mole there were also the soft, sandy beaches stretching for sixteen miles eastwards from Dunkirk to Nieuport that could be used for evacuating the troops – beaches at places such as Malo-les-Bains, Bray-Dunes and La Panne. This image shows Allied troops on one of these beaches forming into long winding queues ready to take their turn to be rescued. (All images Historic Military Press unless stated otherwise)

By the night of 27/28 May, the main bodies of I and II Corps had withdrawn behind the River Lys, leaving a strong rearguard holding the line of the river. The rearguard followed the main columns on the night of 28/29 May.

However, on 28 May, the Belgian Army, trapped by the Germans in what remained of unoccupied Belgium, surrendered. This opened a twenty-mile gap on Gort's eastern front between the British and the sea. At a time when Gort was seeking to reduce the area held by the BEF he had to send the 3rd, 4th and 50th Divisions to plug this gap.

This sudden, though hardly unexpected, capitulation, prompted King George VI to send a supportive telegram to Gort: 'All your countrymen have been following with pride and admiration the courageous resistance of the British Expeditionary Force during the continuing fighting of the last fortnight. Faced by circumstances outside their control in a position of extreme difficulty, they are displaying a gallantry which has never been surpassed in the annals of the British Army. The hearts of everyone of us at home are with you and your magnificent troops in this hour of peril.'[1]

Facing eight German divisions along this eastern perimeter from Nieuport to Ploegsteert (often referred to by the British as 'Plugstreet') were just five British divisions, but the most important sector was in the centre which ran from La Motte through Ploegsteert to Comines which linked the western and eastern fronts. There the French III Corps and the remains of the 1st Army's Cavalry Corps held the middle of this central sector from Estaires to Ploegsteert with the 42nd and 4th divisions of the BEF occupying the left which touched the eastern front. It was to the south of this central front that the most pressure was being exerted by a combined German force of Rommel's 7th Panzers and Bock's 7th Infantry Division.

The situation on the western side of the pocket was a confused one, the Germans having broken through the British line, forcing the 2nd and 44th Divisions to pull back closer to Dunkirk. The 44th Division had lost heavily as it withdrew to Mont des Cats, and the 2nd Division was so badly mauled that its survivors were sent back past Poperinghe to the coast. To add to the confusion, the still only partially-formed III Corps found its component parts cut off from each other by the German advance.

By early morning of the 28th, the leading units of the 1st Panzer Division were only eight miles from Dunkirk and later in the morning Guderian toured round the western front of the perimeter to examine the strength of the Allied positions. He concluded that, 'Further tank attacks would involve useless sacrifice of our best troops.' ▶

Later in the day, the Germans reached Nieuport on the coast just to the north of La Panne, and the German capture of Ostend was confirmed. The net was tightening around the BEF.

Within the Allied pocket, the troops were trying to make their way to Dunkirk as quickly as they could but the traffic on the roads had assumed 'formidable proportions'. Ever since the start of the German offensive on 10 May the French and Belgian civilians had taken to the roads. In the first few days of the fighting, the British troops had been moving in the opposite direction – towards the enemy. But when the BEF withdrew to the Dyle, the traffic problem became acute, as Gort explained in his dispatch of the 28th:

'Refugees began to leave their homes in northern France before the French Government put into operation the plans they had made. The French organisations were not available and no British troops could be spared to control the traffic. The refugee problem had therefore become increasingly acute, and the tide which at first set westwards from Belgium had now met the enemy again in the Somme area and had begun to turn back on itself. Scenes of misery were everywhere, and the distress of women, children and aged people was pitiable. Fortunately, the fine weather and warm nights mitigated their plight to some degree and though the outbreak of famine was expected at any moment it did not actually occur in the area of the B.E.F.

'Little, unfortunately, could be done to help the refugees, since supplies for the troops were still seriously short. Moreover, their presence on the roads was often a grave menace to our movement. It had been necessary to give Corps a free hand in handling them: on occasions, it had been necessary to turn vehicles into the fields in order to keep the roads clear.'

Amongst those that did managed to push his way through the fleeing crowds to reach Dunkirk was Captain Anthony Rhodes of 253 Field Company, Royal Engineers: 'We arrived at Dunkirk on the night of the 27/28 May, and the first sign we had of the town was in the early hours, looking north-west, where we saw an enormous column of black smoke … We picked our way through the centre of Dunkirk, which was under a pall of smoke, with the stink of burning buildings, and vehicles falling to pieces everywhere.'[2]

During the early hours of the 28th, disaster struck out at sea. *Queen of the Channel* had set off from Dunkirk at around 04.00 hours with approximately 950 troops on board. Shortly after leaving the French port, as dawn was breaking, she was attacked by dive bombers.

The bombs fell abaft of the main mast damaging the rudder, breaking the starboard propeller shaft and breaking the ship's back as it lifted out of the water. With the *Queen of the Channel* in serious distress the nearby coaster *Dorrien Rose*, under Captain W. Thompson and carrying military stores to the Dunkirk beaches, approached bow to bow and within thirty-five minutes had taken off the troops from the sinking ship. Also taken in tow were four of *Queen of the Channel*'s lifeboats, though two would later come adrift. *Dorrien Rose* reached Dover at around 14.00 hours.[3]

The damage sustained by *Queen of the Channel* proved fatal and the ship sank that day. The loss of this ship saw daylight operations restricted to naval vessels and the smaller vessels. The larger unarmed vessels were from this time onwards only permitted to operate at night.

LEFT: **A shelter dug on the beach at Dunkirk by Allied troops awaiting evacuation. The picture was taken by a German war photographer after the end of Operation *Dynamo*.**

BELOW: **A picture of the dunes on the beach at Bray-Dunes. The beaches east of Dunkirk can be reached at a variety of locations. One site is the Reserve Naturelle Dune Marchand, a nature reserve to the west of Bray-Dunes. The reserve covers a total of eighty-three acres, and is signposted off the D-60 coast road.** (Courtesy of Arnaud Franoux)

A view of the clouds of dense black smoke that hung over Dunkirk for much of the evacuation. The original caption states that this picture was taken from a Royal Navy destroyer.

It was the naval vessels, and in particular the destroyers, that were now to play the lead role in the evacuation. With his plan to use the East Mole, the destroyers *Mackay*, *Montrose*, *Verity*, *Sabre*, *Worcester* and *Anthony* berthed alongside, where Tennant had organised the rapid flow of men and arranged for berthing parties to help the ships tie up. Once loaded, the destroyers pulled out stern first and then turned for Dover.

HMS *Mackay* had reached Dunkirk at 09.55 hours from the Irish Sea and in the space of just an hour had picked up 600 men from the far end of the Mole. As *Mackay* backed away from the Mole, her berth was taken by *Montrose*. An hour later *Worcester* and *Anthony* arrived and berthed ahead of *Montrose*.

The flow of destroyers, the ships that would eventually become the unsung heroes of the Dunkirk operation, continued. Of these HMS *Sabre*, which had already taken 158 men off the beach at Malo-les-Bains, berthed alongside *Montrose*.

The Eastern Mole was, by this time, crammed with troops, and several German aircraft attempted to bomb the narrow breakwater. But the ships berthed alongside the Mole were no ordinary transports, they were fighting ships, and the destroyers opened up with their light armament, and the enemy 'planes were driven off. The aim of the German aircrew was also hampered by the black smoke from the burning oil

tanks to the east of Dunkirk which drifted over the town and the harbour. To this was added the dazzling flames and air-borne debris from houses that had been bombed along the sea front.

A Lockheed Hudson of Coastal Command's 220 Squadron pictured over the Dunkirk beaches during the evacuation.

The anti-aircraft cruiser HMS *Calcutta* was attacked on its way over to France by a German E-boat, a torpedo flashing just 100 yards passed the ship's stern at 01.25 hours as the cruiser made its way to anchor off La Panne, at around 02.30 hours.

The first supplies of food, water and ammunition from England reached the beaches during the 28th, and were landed at La Panne. Already off the beaches were the paddle-minesweepers, *Sandown* and *Gracie Fields*, as well as the destroyers *Grafton*, *Greyhound* and *Impulsive*. The skoot, *Hebe II*, unable to find any troops to collect from the beaches, went back to Dunkirk and collected 150 men from the East Mole. Clearly there was still a considerable degree of confusion and lack of coordination between ship and shore. In all fairness, as the Admiralty accounts make clear, the flow of troops to any one point could not be known at this early stage in the operation with the various units arriving in piecemeal fashion.

It was, therefore, impossible to regulate the movement of the ships to meet the fluctuating, and unpredictable demand.

At 03.20 hours HMS *Vimy* arrived off the beach at Zuydcoote, some three miles east of Dunkirk, and sent her boats to assist in filling up the minesweeper *Brighton Belle*. Whilst this was underway, the destroyer went to the East Mole and collected 613 soldiers.

Brighton Belle set off for Ramsgate with 350 troops she had plucked off the beach at Zuydcoote, but she came under aerial attack and, in the confusion of trying to avoid the enemy aircraft, at 13.30 hours she struck a submerged wreck off the Gull Light buoy. Sapper Eric Reader had been rescued from the beach and was huddled in the ship's boiler room drying off when the ship rammed into the wreck with a fierce jolt. 'Never touched us,' an old cockney stocker called out cheerfully, Reader recalled. But soon the water started to gurgle into the boat and *Brighton Belle* began to sink. The fearful troops began tumbling up onto the main deck as the boat's hooter blasted out the dots and dashes that signalled SOS. Luckily, *Sandown*, *Medway Queen* and the ex-Belgian canal boat *Yser* were close by.

On 28 May 1940, as part of the Dover Patrol, HMS *Medway Queen* was anchored off the south coast watching out for German aircraft laying mines when she was ordered to make for Dunkirk. *Medway Queen*'s cook was Thomas Russell: ▶

The anti-aircraft cruiser HMS *Calcutta* – one of the largest warships to participate in the evacuation. Though her commander, Captain Dennis Marescaux Lees, described *Calcutta*'s involvement in the evacuation as a 'minor part', she remained in action, and under fire, for much of Operation *Dynamo*, weighing anchor at Sheerness for the last time in the early hours of 3 June. (US Naval History and Heritage Command)

The paddle steamer *Medway Queen* made seven trips to Dunkirk and rescued some 7,000 men. (Photograph by Clem Rutter, www.clemrutter.net)

ABOVE: **A member of *Medway Queen*'s crew pictured beside the 12-pounder gun.** (Courtesy of the Medway Queen Preservation Society)

'One afternoon in May 1940 the *Medway Queen* left Dover for the Continent where our forces were in trouble. A long time before we got there we saw the flames, and soon we smelled the fuel oil. No person who was there will forget it … We had a motor boat which towed another one to and fro from the beach. The army lined up on the shore – I did not see anyone panic or jump the queue … On one trip we came back in company with the

(Courtesy of Nigel Simmons)

One of *Medway Queen*'s restored paddle boxes. Not only is *Medway Queen* one of the most famous of the surviving 'Little Ships', she is also important for the fact that she is the only surviving estuary paddle steamer left in the United Kingdom. Having been threatened with destruction or demolition on a number of occasions since the Second World War, *Medway Queen* was finally saved by the Medway Queen Preservation Society. Through this organisation's efforts this remarkable ship is being restored for future generations. To find out about the Medway Queen Preservation Society's efforts to restore the paddle steamer to her former glory, or how to visit her at Gillingham Pier, see: www.medwayqueen.co.uk.

Brighton Belle; she hit a wreck … we went alongside and they all came aboard before she sank. Fortunately, it was a calm day as we were very overloaded, but we got home okay.'[4]

Everyone on board was taken off – even the captain's dog.[5] If such losses as this could be contained in this way, then there was real hope that something quite extraordinary just might be possible.

Thomas Russell also wrote of what happened when the paddle steamer reached the UK: 'When the ship returned to Ramsgate, ladies were waiting with tea and sandwiches and our passengers were whisked away. We refuelled, stored, tidied up and it was time to go again.'

PERMISSION TO SURRENDER

At 11.00 hours, Général Blanchard went to Gort's headquarters at Houtkerque. There Gort read out his orders to evacuate the BEF. Blanchard had not been informed by his government of the British decision and he was mortified to hear that the British were abandoning him. He was even more upset to learn that Weygand had known of the British evacuation two days earlier and had not told Blanchard of this, or of the agreement with the French Government that French 1st Army would withdraw to Dunkirk to both help defend the perimeter and to evacuate as many French troops as possible.

Blanchard protested that his men were too worn out to withdraw any further and that, in any case, he would never abandon France. Gort wrote in his despatch to London, how he tried to persuade the French general: 'I then begged General Blanchard, for the sake of France, the French Army and the Allied Cause to order General Prioux [who commanded the French 1st Army's Cavalry Corps] back. Surely, I said, his troops were not so tired as to be incapable of moving. The French Government would be able to provide ships for at least some of his troops, and that the chance of saving part of his trained soldiers was preferable to the certainty of losing them all.'

Blanchard would have none of it. Evacuation from open beaches was impossible and would only lead to an even greater disaster than trying to stand and fight the enemy. Gort concluding his despatch with the following terse sentence: 'I could not move him.'

During the afternoon of the 28th Gort shifted his headquarters to a building in La Panne. This not only enabled him to be closer to the evacuation beaches, but there was a direct telephone link with London. It was there where King Albert of Belgium had his headquarters during the First World War. Gort received a briefing on the current state of affairs from General Adam and the

BELOW: **The stricken paddle steamer *Brighton Belle* pictured sinking after having struck the submerged wreck of a recently-mined ship on 28 May 1940. Considered to be a 'small and slow steamer', *Brighton Belle* had just picked up some 800 soldiers at Dunkirk.** (Courtesy of the Medway Queen Preservation Society)

HMS *Medway Queen*'s wartime crew pictured with the ship's dog. In view of *Medway Queen*'s remarkable achievement in rescuing so many Allied troops from France during Operation *Dynamo*, she was given the nickname of 'The Heroine of Dunkirk'.
(Courtesy of the Medway Queen Preservation Society)

Quartermaster General, Lieutenant General W.G. Laidsell: 'No ships could be unloaded at the docks at Dunkirk, and few wounded could be evacuated. There was no water in Dunkirk and very little on the beaches, 10,000 [men] having been taken off in the last two days, chiefly from Dunkirk.' Adam, though, remained positive, saying that 'given a reasonable measure of immunity from air attack, troops could gradually be evacuated … If, however, intensive air attacks continued the beaches might easily become a shambles within the next forty-eight hours.'[6]

Gort duly passed this information on to London, asking what course of action he should take if indeed the beaches became a killing ground. He received the following reply from the Chief of the Imperial General Staff, General Edmund Ironside: 'H.M. Govt. fully approve your withdrawal to extricate your force in order to embark maximum possible of B.E.F. If you are cut from all communication with us, and all evacuation from Dunkirk and beaches had, in your judgement, been finally prevented after every attempt to re-open it had failed you would become sole judge of when it was impossible to inflict further damage to the enemy.'

The wording of this message could have only one meaning; that Gort had been given permission to surrender, but the decision if and when the BEF should put down its arms rested solely with him. Such is the burden of leadership.

It was on the afternoon of the 28th that Général Blanchard, went to Gort's new headquarters. He had evidently spent the day pondering over Gort's appeal to him earlier in the day, and had seen the wisdom of the British commander's words. It was hard for him to accept not just that the French Army was collapsing but that its defeat was so complete that there was no alternative but to leave the country. Blanchard consented, agreeing that part of the French 1st Army would withdraw to within the Dunkirk perimeter on 30 May.

THE 'LITTLE SHIPS'

It was on the 28th, that the first of the 'Little Ships' reached Dunkirk. The various boatyards that had been searched by the men from the Admiralty had yielded upwards of forty serviceable motor-boats or launches, which were assembled at Sheerness.

At the same time lifeboats from liners in the London docks, yachts, fishing-craft, lighters, barges and pleasure-boats, coasting vessels, skoots, motor boats and other small craft – including rowing boats for inshore work off the beaches – were called into service. The final total of these Little Ships amounted to some 1,300, though the exact number is not known.

Lieutenant Dann RN sailed with the first convoy of this motley collection of boats: 'The first assembly was typical of the whole of this miniature armada. A dozen or so motor yachts from 20 to fifty feet in length, nicely equipped and smartly maintained by proud individual owners, a cluster of cheap 'conversion jobs', mainly the work of amateur craftsmen, who had set to work in their spare time to convert a ship's lifeboat or any old half discarded hull into a cabin cruiser of sorts …[and] half a dozen Thames river launches resembling nothing so much as the upper decks of elongated motorbuses with their rows of slatted seats … The very names of these latter craft are redolent of the quiet of Richmond, Teddington and Hampton Court: *Skylark*, *Elizabeth* and *Queen Boadicea*. A strange flotilla indeed to be taking an active part in what has been described as the greatest naval epic in history.'[7]

Once they arrived off the beaches many of the boats remained there to transport the troops from the shore to the waiting ships anchored in deeper water. Harry Brown and Fred Hook represented the crew of one of those vessels, a small motor boat from Deal called *Gypsy King*. Its skipper, A. Betts, submitted the following report:

'We went to Dunkirk on May 28th. We stayed there about forty-eight hours. We ▶

ABOVE: *Medway Queen* stands by the fatally damaged *Brighton Belle*. Fortunately, thanks to the efforts of the crew of *Medway Queen* all the soldiers onboard *Brighton Belle* were rescued, along with its crew and the Captain's dog. (Courtesy of the Medway Queen Preservation Society)

The remains of a French anti-aircraft position located beside the D2 immediately south of Dunkirk and a short distance east from the Canal de Bergues. Constructed in 1939, this battery of four raised concrete emplacements was manned by the men of Batterie No.201 of the 406e Regiment d'Artillerie de DCA. It was one of eight such sites supporting the air defence system for the Dunkirk area. Equipped with 75mm guns on semi-fixed platforms, the battery was in action throughout the evacuations, being mentioned in despatches by Admiral Abrial on 28 May 1940. On 2 June Abrial ordered that the guns and emplacements be destroyed to prevent their use by the rapidly approaching Germans.

ABOVE: **British troops boarding another of the many Royal Navy warships involved in Operation** *Dynamo*, **in this case the V-class destroyer HMS** *Vanquisher*, **from the Mole at Dunkirk at low tide.**

they kept in line, and no-one tried to steal a march on anyone else. Most of them even managed to summon up an occasional joke or wisecrack.'

A somewhat different picture of the situation on the beaches was given by Private Reg Rymer, serving in the 2nd Battalion, the Cheshire Regiment: 'Obviously, the main job was to get out to the boats. Because when we finally decided to come down out of the ... sand dunes ... you've got to remember, we're running across the beach, and you're jumping over blokes, you know, that are no longer with us, sort of thing. And dodging and diving, because they're [the Luftwaffe] coming down, machine gunning you, and everything else. You're trying to keep an eye on there, and there's another one coming that way.'

For much of the 28th though, all of the available destroyers were working off the beaches east of Dunkirk using their own boats as most of the 'Little Ships' were still en route. A moderate surf on the beaches reduced the rate of embarkation, exhausting the boats' crews, the majority of whom were 'hostility only' ratings, rendering the whole operation slow and difficult.

There could only be a matter of another day or so before the Germans broke through and the embarkation had to be speeded up if even the estimate of 45,000 men were to be saved. Ramsay approached the Admiralty to see what could be done, and, accordingly, the Commander-in-Chief, Western Approaches and Commander-in-Chief, Portsmouth, were instructed to sail every available destroyer to Dover. In addition, the 7th and 8th Minesweeper Flotillas were ordered to Harwich and a patrol of all available Motor Torpedo Boats and anti-submarine trawlers were ordered to cover the north-east flank of the evacuation area against attack by enemy surface craft from the north. It seemed as if the Admiralty had suddenly woken to the plight Britain was in, with its only army stranded on the Continent, and at last every effort was being made to rescue the BEF.

Captain Tennant signaled his evacuation plan for the coming night to the S.N.O. Dover at 15.55 hours. This allowed for three Hospital Carriers, seven ferries/packets and two destroyers to embark from the East Mole, while twenty destroyers, nineteen minesweepers, seventeen drifters, twenty-four

were under shell-fire and machine-gun fire. We stayed there till every British soldier was off the beach. I would like to mention Harry Brown who did a brave action. We just loaded [the] boat with troops. We saw a pontoon with soldiers in, being swamped with waves. Brown, being the swimmer, decided to go over the side with a rope, he tied it to the pontoon and saved the soldiers from being drowned.'

As the day progressed, the build-up of troops on the beaches exceeded the capacity of the ships, large and small, to recover them, and long lines of desperate, but patient soldiers, began to form:

'There they stood, lined up like a bus queue, right from the dunes, down the shore, to the water's edge, and sometimes up to their waists beyond. They were as patient and orderly, too, as people in an ordinary bus queue. There were bombers overhead and artillery fire all around them. They were hungry and thirsty and dead-beat; yet

The original caption to this vertical aerial reconnaissance photograph states that it is 'a remarkable aerial photograph of part of the BEF on the sand dunes and foreshore at Dunkirk waiting to be evacuated. The picture shows about 700 yards of the beach about four miles east of the town. Three hundred to four hundred men are to be seen on the beach, while one or two small rowing boats and a wrecked lighter are lying off shore.'

BELOW: **British and French troops wade through shallow water to a skoot beached on the sands east of Dunkirk.**

ABOVE: **German troops advancing towards Dunkirk pass abandoned vehicles.**

ABOVE: **The Hospital Ship *St David* at Dunkirk during Operation *Dynamo*.**

ABOVE: **An aerial photograph of evacuation vessels of all shapes and sizes off Dunkirk during Operation *Dynamo*.**

skoots, five coastal ships, twelve motor boats, two tugs, twenty-eight pulling cutters and lifeboats were to operate in an area from a point one-and-a-half miles east of Dunkirk to as far as La Panne.

THE LOSSES MOUNT

The Armed Boarding Vessel *King Orry* arrived at Dunkirk harbour at about 19.00 hours to find it occupied with nothing other than burning and sinking ships. She soon came under air attack. She was an easy target, and was hit, with her steering gear being put out of action and all her instruments shattered. As she lay there more German 'planes attacked, the bombs dropping frighteningly close, causing further damage. Seeing that if *King Orry* was sunk, the channel would be blocked, Captain Tennant instructed her to get out of the harbour. It would prove a long and difficult task, one that *King Orry* would not survive.

About the same time that *King Orry* was being bombed, the minesweeper HMS *Halcyon* witnessed what appeared to be the deliberate bombing of the Hospital Carrier *Isle*

of Guernsey. She was attacked by ten German aircraft off Dunkirk whilst attempting to pick up a downed airman. Although damaged by near misses, *Isle of Guernsey* entered the harbour after dark and embarked 490 wounded over the course of many hours. The airman was rescued by *Halcyon*.

HMS *Grenade* was also hit by bombs and sank; the trawler *Calvi* suffered a similar fate. The sloop *Bideford* anchored off Bray beach at 17.30 hours and twenty minutes later the first boat loads of troops (mostly French) came alongside. The event was recorded by her skipper, Lieutenant Commander J.H. Lewes:

'The boats were dangerously overcrowded and several swamped on the way off from the shore. On arrival alongside, the men would all jump on board and let their boats drift off on the tide. Paddles were lost overboard, rendering the boats useless. *Bideford*'s M/B was lowered and ordered to collect and tow inshore any empty boats. The whaler was lowered and 2 officers and a signalman were sent in to endeavor to take charge on the beach … this was next to impossible. The men rushed the boats and capsized them

in shallow water, and then left the boats without making any attempt to right them and use them again. There were only 2 motor landing craft in the vicinity. One had one engine out of action; the other [*A.L.C. 16*] was blown up subsequently when laying alongside the ship.'[8]

At around 19.00 hours *Bideford* was the target of Stukas. She was then machine-gunned at low level and, a few minutes later, was bombed again. One bomb landed just thirty yards away and another hit the stern, detonating one of the sloop's depth charges. About forty feet of *Bideford*'s stern was blown away and a further forty feet was reduced to tangled mass of metal. The main mast was blown down, wrecking the searchlight and the machine-gun platform. The bridge superstructure was damaged as were other parts of the sloop. Two officers and thirteen men of the crew were killed and a further nineteen wounded, with the troops on board also having two officers and ten men killed and two officers wounded.

The evacuation of the BEF was going as badly as many feared it would. ✦

LEFT: **British soldiers wade out to a small launch from a beach near Dunkirk. Realistic though this photograph appears, it was in fact taken during the production of the war film *Dunkirk* which was released in 1958. Records suggest that none of the 'Little Ships' that participated in *Dynamo* were named *Vanity*, though one motor launch named *Vanitee*, owned by D.V. Johnson, did cross the Channel but failed to return.**

NOTES:
1. Quoted in Basil Liddell Hart, *History of the Second World War* (Putmam, New York, 1970), p.41.
2. Quoted in Joshua Levine, *Forgotten Voices of Dunkirk* (Edbury Press, 2010), pp.237 and 249.
3. Dr John Rickard, *Operation Dynamo, the evacuation from Dunkirk, 27 May-4 June 1940*, http://www.historyofwar.org/articles/operation_dynamo.html
4. Quoted on the *Medway Queen* website: www.medwayqueen.co.uk.
5. Walter Lord, *The Miracle of Dunkirk* (Allen Lane, London, 1982), p.117.
6. Gardner, p.26.
7. Lieutenant A. Dann's report, TNA ADM 199/788.
8. Gardner, p.45.

Throughout the course of the 28th, 5,390 men were landed in the UK from the beaches to the east of Dunkirk and 11,874 from the harbour and the East Mole. With the 7,669 landed on the 27th. This meant that just 24,933 men had been rescued so far, little more than half of the total the Admiralty had estimated the Royal Navy could save. But the perimeter was holding, offering the prospect of extending the operation and, at last, the Admiralty was committing every available resource to *Dynamo*.

With agreement having been reached with Général Blanchard, the French 1st Army was also withdrawing towards Dunkirk and participating in holding back the Germans. This enabled the BEF's I and II Corps to disengage from the enemy and withdraw into the Dunkirk perimeter, III Corps, being the least advanced, having already reached La Panne.

Large numbers of Blanchard's troops were also entering the perimeter, bringing with them a great deal of their transport. 'The congestion created within the perimeter was well-nigh unbearable,' complained Gort, 'and for two days the main road between La Panne and Dunkirk became totally blocked with vehicles three deep'.

The arrival of the French troops came as a great surprise to Admiral Abrial who had not been informed by his Government either that efforts would be made to try and save the entire BEF or that French soldiers would also be evacuated. This meant that no evacuation plan had been drawn up for the French and there were no French ships waiting to receive the troops. Naturally, the French that were now piling into the already crowded beaches expected to be taken off in the same proportion as their British allies. The potential for trouble was obvious, and so until Abrial could arrange for transport, Gort allocated two ships to the French troops, so that they could see they were not being willfully left behind.

Amongst those French troops was Marceau Lantenois of the 2nd Company, 43rd Battalion, First Regiment of Engineers:

'We left for Dunkirk and Malot. We rode either by car or on foot. There were scores of bombing raids there as well, all along the road. It was terrible. We were shelled heavily. I lost some comrades and even cried there. Good comrades who were left by the road.

'Well, after that, I think I arrived in Dunkirk. No, it was not Dunkirk, it was Malot, Malot-les-Bains. I remember it was Malot because we hid ourselves in a casino when the bombs were falling. It was a sad place, Dunkirk. Everything had been devastated; there was smoke and all that. There was even a woman crying - she had lost her mind because of the bombing.

'We got into the Casino, to protect ourselves from the bombs as well, but we didn't know where to go. And, on the beach, there were the dead. Some of them had holes in their heads. And on the sea, it was horrible. Boats were

DAY 4: 29 MAY

In the first days of Operation *Dynamo* only small numbers of men had been rescued but the situation was beginning to change.

The scene on the beach at La Panne in a photograph taken from outside the Hotel Splendide by Sub-Lieutenant John Rutherford Crosby, a member of the crew of the minesweeper, and converted Clyde paddle steamer, HMS *Oriole*. Both *Oriole* (left of centre) and a Dutch skoot, seen above the back of the abandoned car, are beached. Vessels standing offshore include the paddle minesweeper *Waverley* (on the right), another skoot and several Royal Navy destroyers. (All images Historic Military Press unless stated otherwise)

sinking all around. There were some of which we could see only the mast. And planes were falling into the water.'[1]

As the men withdrew to Dunkirk, they were ordered not to allow equipment to fall into enemy hands, which astonished Corporal George Ledger of the 8th Battalion, Durham Light Infantry: 'When we got to the outskirts of Dunkirk, we came upon a whole consignment of dumped arms, lorries and equipment; miles and miles of it. Wherever you looked, the whole place was engulfed with abandoned weapons and machines. A lot of us were sent out to immobilise some of the vehicles. We'd put things into the radiators, or drop a grenade in and smash it.'[2]

Corporal Bob Bloom also remarked the mass of abandoned and destroyed equipment: 'The road to Dunkirk was littered with the cast-off equipment of a modern army. Nothing too big, nothing too small, it was all there. The army vehicles, which we had left behind, were to be burned to deny their use to the enemy. There was sufficient equipment to keep an army and navy store supplied for a hundred years or more! There were vehicles of all kinds, large artillery pieces, with their barrels spiked, to lightweight tanks sticking up out of the waterways. The sight of all these valuable military pieces was depressing to us, and told the story of an army routed and defeated. ▶

ABOVE: Soldiers wait patiently in line, up to their necks in the sea, to be hauled aboard HMS *Oriole*, which had been beached at La Panne, 29 May 1940. Though it is one of the most widely published pictures of the evacuation, rarely, if ever, has the photographer, Sub-Lieutenant Crosby, been credited. It is also on occasion been described as a fake – a montage – on the assumption that no ship could get so far inshore without running aground.

RIGHT: The original caption to this picture states that it shows 'British soldiers helping comrades board a River Clyde paddle steamer in the early dawn during the evacuation of the BEF'. It is almost certainly another of the images taken by Sub-Lieutenant John Crosby from HMS *Oriole*.

'Soon we were entering the main port of Dunkirk, which appeared to be largely in flames and the dismal sound of collapsing buildings reverberated through the empty streets. It appeared there had just been an air raid. Dunkirk was in ruins. The roads were cratered everywhere and tram lines stood on end where the many bombs had landed. The corpses of mutilated soldiers lay everywhere and the smell of burning flesh was nauseating.'

It was evident that the British were abandoning France, but the German Army was not prepared to sit and let the Luftwaffe finish off the BEF, and throughout the 29th they attempted to cross the canal between the French-Belgian frontier and Nieuport. At the latter location, where the bridge had not been blown, they established a bridgehead in the town. Everywhere else they were driven back. Some attempted to cross in rubber boats; others were disguised as civilians, even allegedly as nuns, and attempted to cross with the refugees. Though the perimeter was holding, the Germans were now close enough for their artillery to reach Dunkirk and the beaches, and their shelling added to the death and destruction wrought by the Luftwaffe.

The perimeter, nevertheless, was holding, and the evacuation was progressing much

RIGHT: British troops rescued from Dunkirk disembarking in a South Coast port during Operation *Dynamo*. These soldiers have arrived on the Isle of Man Steam Packet Co. vessel *Tynwald*, and are crossing the decks of another steam packet vessel, probably *Ben-my-Chree*, to land at the Admiralty Pier at Dover.

faster than at any previous time. Operating early off the beaches was the paddle steamer *Medway Queen*. As might be gathered from her name, *Medway Queen* had been employed on the River Medway and the Thames Estuary before being requisitioned by the Admiralty and fitted out as a minesweeper. She was ordered to take station off La Panne, having towed some small motor boats over from England, to collect men from the beach. As dawn broke on the 29th the crew sent in the boats, time and time again, to load up as many men as they could carry. By 07.00 hours the *Medway Queen* had taken on board around 1,000 men and she set off back across the Channel.

By 17.00 hours on the 29th, what was left of the flotilla of paddle steamers that had made the round trip from France, lined up to cross the Channel once again. This time Lieutenant Thomas Cook RNR was ordered to take troops from the Mole, as *Medway Queen*'s First Officer, Sub Lieutenant John Graves RNR, remembered: 'Off the entrance the flotilla came under very heavy fire from shore batteries, and some of the ships hauled out of the line as the sea spouted columns of water around them. The scene was awe inspiring. Rows of great oil tanks were blazing furiously and the glare was reflected on the clouds.

'Heavy shells plunged into the harbour which was littered with wrecks. It was enough to daunt the stoutest navigator but still the ships came and went, feeling their way past uncharted obstructions and avoiding each other.'

The ships tied up against the Mole and men had to climb down ladders to reach the decks of the paddle steamer, several feet below. 'It was while we were tied to the Mole that we were most vulnerable," said

RIGHT: A remarkable shot of the beach at La Panne during a German air raid. It was taken from the decks of HMS *Oriole*, once again by Sub-Lieutenant Crosby; he had turned and captured the very moment that a pair of German bombs fell on the sands and exploded.

ABOVE LEFT: HMS *Wakeful* pictured at speed off Dunkirk prior to her loss.

The personnel vessel *Tynwald* passes the wreck of her Steam Packet sister, *King Orry*, as she approaches Dunkirk on 29 May 1940.

RIGHT: One of the 'Little Ships' pictured in its peacetime role. This is the Southend pleasure boat *Princess Maud* providing a good illustration of how just many people could be carried. Accompanied by other Southend pleasure boats, *Princess Maud* crossed to Dunkirk on 29 May 1940, but ran aground and was lost after getting too close inshore.

BELOW: At about 01.00 hours on 29 May, the destroyer HMS *Wakeful*, seen here, was attacked by German E-boats, being hit by a torpedo fired by *E-30*. *Wakeful* broke in two and sank in just fifteen seconds.

the *Medway Queen*'s signaler, Eric Woodroffe. 'There was much more enemy activity then. I remember the bombs coming down, other ships being hit including a cruiser, and getting the soldiers on board as fast as we could.'

One of those rescued by *Medway Queen* was Alf George, of Ashford, Kent, who served with the Royal Artillery: 'There were stretchers and bodies all along the Mole as we made our way along. We were given a tin of bully beef and a big packet of hard biscuits and told to share it among five of us. We'd been without food for three days. I looked over and there was this little paddle steamer about six feet below me. A sailor helped me down and I went to the after cabin and sat on a bench seat where I dropped off to sleep. Then I was woken up by an airburst of shell fire. I looked out of the window and there were all these flashes.

'The floor was completely covered with stretchers and injured men. I slept again and was awoken by a shuddering and a rattling, then everything went quiet. We thought we would be taken back across to France to continue fighting, but instead we were taken to Ramsgate Pier and unloaded. There were people at the end of the pier all cheering us.'

On being informed by Lord Gort that III Corps had reached La Panne, Ramsay ordered all destroyers and light craft to that end of the beach to make a concerted effort to recover these troops. The cruiser *Calcutta* was off La Panne and she used her boats to lift 1,200 troops off the beach. At just before 14.00 hours, she set off for Sheerness. The captain of *Calcutta* had sent a boat to pick up Lord Gort, but the general 'courteously refused' to leave his men.

As well as the destroyers, also operating off La Panne were five drifters, three motor launches, the minesweepers *Sutton* and *Salamanca* and the tug *Java*. Together these vessels saved 6,652 men, in a large part of

which was down to the paddle steamer *Oriole* which beached herself at La Panne to act as a form of pier to which the other vessels could go alongside. The soldiers were able to climb onto *Oriole*, and move across its decks to the waiting ships.

RESCUING THE FRENCH

It was on the 29th that many of the 'Little Ships' began to arrive off the beaches. This included six Assault Landing Craft which had been carried across the Channel on the SS *Clan Macalister*. Three of these, *ALC 5*, *16* and *17*, were swamped by desperate French troops. As soon as *ALC 5* reached the shore it was 'rushed on all sides by French soldiers, so many of them got on board that the boat grounded'. It was only when some of them had been pushed off, that the boat could be refloated.

Sub Lieutenant R.O. Wilcoxon RNVR, in command of *ALC 15*, had an even worse experience: 'She was boarded by French soldiers, who overwhelmed the boat to such an extent that she became partially swamped,

and the starboard battery was flooded and both engines failed.' Again, it was only by evicting some of the Frenchmen that one of the engines could be started. But the boat was damaged when going astern and water poured into the landing craft. *ALC 15* was kept afloat only by constant pumping and bailing she continued to operate, taking off some 600 men.

ALC 17, likewise, was grounded by French troops and remained stuck on the beach for three hours. When the tide flooded in and the boat began to float, the French troops made another rush for her, and it was only thanks to some British soldiers who drove the French away, that the landing craft was able to get off the beach. *ALC 17* then ferried troops to the waiting ships all day and throughout the night until her engines broke down.

The story was the same for one of the first motor boats to reach France, *Scenceshifter*. Rushed by French troops, she too was swamped – to such a degree that she sunk, becoming a total loss. ▶

Such was the scale of the disaster that only twenty-five of *Wakeful*'s crew and one evacuee were saved. The corvette HMS *Sheldrake* sank the wreck the following day leaving *Wakeful* and those who perished on board in the shallow waters of the Channel as a war grave. In 2001, following an agreement by the British and Belgian authorities, work began to deal with the danger that *Wakeful*'s wreck, lying at a depth of just fifty-three feet, presented to the modern deep-draught ships that use the English Channel. It was eventually decided to remove part of HMS *Wakeful*'s superstructure, including funnels and navigation equipment, and secure them to the side of the wreck. It was during this sensitive operation that the tread-plate seen here was recovered by Belgian divers. (Courtesy of Robert Mitchell)

LEFT: **Sub-Lieutenant Crosby was undoubtedly busy with his camera during HMS *Oriole*'s time on the beach at La Panne. This is almost certainly another of his views. Requisitioned by the Admiralty, PS *Eagle III* left the Clyde in early 1940, having been renamed HMS *Oriole*, initially for wartime minesweeping duties at Harwich.**

A DEFEATED ARMY

Arriving overnight, the situation on the beaches on the 29th shocked Norman Wickman of 62 Chemical Warfare Company RE: 'With twilight approaching, our small group of four stepped onto the beach at Bray-Dunes. Tens of thousands of exhausted troops congregated on the golden sands with not a spark of fight left in them. Other soldiers formed long lines out to sea. Only their determination to reach home, a mere 22 miles across the English Channel, kept them waiting patiently for rescue boats. They stood chest deep in water, oily and slick from the shipwrecks offshore. Here and there, a body floated, a remnant of the human cargo lost to German bombs. An occasional victim of strafing and shelling littered the sand. The sickly-sweet stench of death lingered in the still air.

'I surveyed the beach, trying to make sense of the scenario before me. Slowly, understanding dawned. Disbelief, horror, then anger welled up, followed by intense shame. Until that moment, I had believed we were an Army in retreat. Now, I realized, I belonged to a defeated army. My pride fought against accepting this fact. I still had plenty of fight left, but looking again at the thousands of dejected men, I could see these soldiers had had it. I was filled with confusion and despair.'[4]

Wickman did not need to despair, for by early afternoon there were fourteen ships lying off Dunkirk. This included six trawlers from the Dover Minesweeping Command, which were sent to the East Mole. The number of ships now involved in Operation *Dynamo* meant that as soon as one ship cast off another swept in to take its berth. When the SS *Lochgarry* pulled away for England with 1,000 men on board, her place was immediately taken by the six trawlers which triple-banked against the Mole.

Six motor yachts also reached La Panne and began towing the ships' whalers out to the anchored ships. Amongst the latter was the yacht *Viewfinder*, which was dragged around by Belgian soldiers and it too became a total loss. As other motor boats arrived they began to play an increasingly important part in the operation, travelling forwards and backwards between ship and shore.

The General Steam Navigation Company's MV *Bullfinch*, a small (432-ton gross) coaster, was deployed at La Panne on the 29th. One of its crewmen was a gunner, Albert Atkinson of 237 Battery, 60th Field Regiment, Royal Artillery: 'As the troops had come on board they were asked to empty their .303 ammunition out of their pouches into a six-foot galvanized bath, before being sent below for shelter, as the Germans were attacking almost non-stop.' The only people allowed to remain on deck

were Albert, who was armed with a Bren gun, and his two magazine-loaders. Once they had prepared around fifty magazines for the gun, Albert sent them below. When the Luftwaffe flew in, Albert rested his Bren on the ship's lifeboat davits – and fired. He claimed two Stukas, which crashed into the sea, and a third which was seen flying away trailing smoke and losing altitude.[3]

ABOVE MIDDLE: **Sub-Lieutenant Crosby took this snapshot of HMS *Oriole*'s gun crew whilst at La Panne. Writing after the conclusion of Dynamo, *Oriole*'s captain, Lieutenant (Temporary) E.L. Davies RNVR, made the following observation on Crosby: 'On several occasions very gallantly and at his own obvious imminent peril dove into surf and tide (strong) to render assistance to soldiers in difficulties and was thereby responsible in preserving many lives.' After Dunkirk, Crosby continued to serve on minesweepers, but was killed in action off the North Africa coast in 1943.**

BELOW: **Amongst the many 'Little Ships' at Dunkirk were vessels of the Minesweeping Service. These men are pictured safe on the deck of the drifter *Fidget* during Operation *Dynamo*.**

LEFT: **The Royal Navy's submarine tender HMS *Dwarf* pictured during the Second World War. Commanded by Sub-Lieutenant D.A. Hare, *Dwarf* was normally based at Gosport as part of the 5th Submarine Flotilla. Having sailed from Portsmouth at 21.00 hours on 29 May, she arrived at Ramsgate at 17.00 hours the next day. After provisioning, coaling and embarking two Lewis guns, *Dwarf* sailed for Dunkirk at 20.00 hours on the 30th, using route 'X'.**

RIGHT: **One of the many 'Little Ships' lost during *Dynamo*. Here German troops are pictured on the wreck of *Beverley* (61A) after the end of the evacuation. Owned by F. Robinson, *Beverley* was reported as having sunk off La Panne.**

A DAY OF LOSSES

Day 4 of Operation *Dynamo* was one of heavy losses amongst the Royal Navy ships and the civilian vessels. In the first hour of the 29th, the destroyer *Wakeful* became the first of only two ships sunk by German E-boats. She was returning to Dover with approximately 650 troops when a torpedo hit her forward of the boiler room. She broke in half and went down in fifteen seconds. Most of those on board went down to the bottom with her.

The bombing was intense. The destroyer *Anthony* was holed by a near miss, which also put her steering gear out of action. She drifted helplessly, listing severely to port, until another destroyer, *Express* came to her rescue, taking off her passengers and towing her to Dover.

After dropping off the landing craft, *Clan Macalister* was bombed and sank in shallow water, her upper structures remaining above the surface. She continued to serve, even though abandoned, as the German bombers thought that she was still afloat and continued to waste their bombs on her.

Others amongst those lost was the steam packet SS *Frenella* which came under aerial attack as she was loading troops from the East Mole. She had more than 600 on board when she was hit by three bombs in quick succession, the first bomb hitting her directly on the promenade deck, the second bomb hitting the Mole, blowing lumps of concrete through the ship's side below the waterline, and the third exploded between the pier and the ship's side, wrecking the engine room. *Frenella* was clearly unable to move, and likely to sink, so the troops were disembarked back onto the Mole. Luckily, the paddle steamer *Crested Eagle* was nearby and the troops were re-embarked.

Crested Eagle duly set off back for the UK. One of those on board was Sergeant W. Clarke of the RAMC who had in his care a number of injured men – including Private

C.T. Newell: 'We were about half a mile out when we were hit by incendiaries and fire rapidly gained control of one end of the ship. A cry then came from the upper deck, "Get the wounded on top". Pte. Newell, in company with several other disabled men, was then dragged up through the hatchway but the press and throng of the crowd was so great that I was unable to keep with him, nor did I see how the wounded were eventually disposed of.

'It was some considerable time afterwards (I think about 15 minutes) before, through the smoke and falling woodwork, I myself managed to gain the upper deck. The boat was, by this time, well ablaze and I had to jump into the water and swim about 200 yards before finally being picked up by the minesweeper *Oldbury*. I never saw Pte. Newell after he left me on the lower deck.'[5] Forty-two-year-old Private 534973 Charles Newell, from Fulham, did not survive. His

body was never found or identified and he is commemorated on the Dunkirk Memorial.

Second Lieutenant F.E. McMaster of the Royal Signals had a fortunate escape from the sinking paddle-steamer: 'I was at the left and the bottom of the staircase when I heard the A.A. machine-guns firing and suddenly the explosion of the first bomb. Instinctively I bent myself as much as possible, protecting my eyes with my hands. Then I heard a terrific noise, saw a big flash, fell down on the back, and fainted. I recovered after a few seconds and was expecting the sinking of the boat. My hands and my face were terribly burnt. The staircase near me was destroyed and all around me some soldiers were killed or wounded trying to extinguish the flames off their burning clothes.

'Then I saw a window on [the] port side and managed to drop myself through it and fell down on a small triangular deck between the side and the left wheel of the paddler. There I recovered with the fresh air and saw that the *Crested Eagle* had been set on fire but the engine was still running. A short time later she was beached near the French shore.[6]

Crested Eagle was hit by four bombs and, as Lieutenant McMaster observed, she was set on fire but her engines kept on running out of control. The destroyer HMS *Verity* signaled for the paddle-steamer to stop so that she could transfer her passengers, but *Crested Eagle* could not stop, and, blazing from fore to stern, she ran aground to the west of Bray beach. The 200 or so survivors in the water were machine-gunned by the Luftwaffe, some being picked up by the minesweepers *Lydd* and *Hebe*.

In this latest German attack, the Southern Railway Steam Ship *Normania* was also hit off Dunkirk. She was towed clear of the Dunkirk channel by the gunboat *Mosquito*, her crew and the troops on board being taken off by the minesweeper *Ross*. *Normania* sank at 02.45 hours on the morning of the 30th. ▶

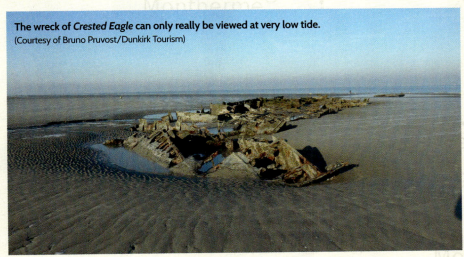

The wreck of *Crested Eagle* can only really be viewed at very low tide.
(Courtesy of Bruno Pruvost/Dunkirk Tourism)

The paddle steamer *Gracie Fields* returned to Dunkirk on her second trip and took off four British officers and some 800 other ranks from La Panne. She set off back for the UK at around 18.00 hours. She did not get far. Whilst still in sight of land she was attacked by enemy bombers and hit amidships. One bomb penetrated the engine room but did not hole the ship. Her steering was also jammed at 15 degrees starboard.

As with *Crested Eagle*, her skipper, Captain N.R. Larkin, was unable to stop *Gracie Fields*' engines and she started going round in circles at six knots. Fortunately, the skoot *Twente* was on its way back from La Panne with 275 French troops on board. The skipper was able to secure his ship alongside *Gracie Fields* – an act of considerable skill – and received as many of the wounded and others as he could. Another skoot, *Jutland*, then secured itself on the other side of the paddle-steamer and took off some more of the men. Finally, the rest of the soldiers were rescued by the minesweeper *Pangbourne*. It was at approximately 18.30 hours that the last man was taken off *Gracie Fields*. The rescue of the men from *Gracie Fields* had taken just thirty minutes. What is equally astonishing is that *Pangbourne* had been holed on both sides above and below the waterline when off Bray beach, having had thirteen men killed and eleven others wounded in the same air attack that saw *Gracie Fields* damaged. After taking eighty men off *Gracie Fields*, *Pangbourne* took the paddle-steamer in tow, but she did not reach England, sinking in mid-Channel.

WAKE-WALKER ARRIVES

Day 4 of Operation *Dynamo* saw twenty-four vessels sunk and another twelve severely damaged and put out of action, but it was a day of remarkable achievement. Altogether, 13,752 men were taken off the beaches and 33,558 from the harbour and the East Mole.

ABOVE: This pair of shipping line-issued binoculars is believed to have been used by the captain of *Crested Eagle*, Lieutenant Commander B.R. Booth, having been recovered from the location of the wreck of this paddle steamer on the beach at Dunkirk. Today, the binoculars are one of the many exhibits in the excellent Mémorial du Souvenir museum in what was Bastion 32 in Dunkirk. (Courtesy of Jules Hudson)

This made a total of 47,310 men landed in the UK on 29 May. It may be recalled that the Admiralty had originally estimated the most that they were likely to be able to save would be 45,000. This figure had been exceeded on one day alone. The total recovered from France now amounted to 72,783.

Amongst the last ships to reach France on the 29th was the skoot *Patria*, which arrived off Bray from Ramsgate at 23.00 hours. Her skipper decided that the quickest way to embark troops off the beach was, like HMS *Oriole*, to run her aground and hope that her engines could pull her off as the tide rose: 'The troops, holding hands, waded out and clambered on board by nets, ladders and ropes' ends. The sight of two solid phalanxes of men, delineated by phosphorescence in the water and steadily advancing to the ship will be memorable … over 1,000 men were embarked in just over two hours.'[7]

This exemplified the manner in which the sailors were going beyond the call of duty to rescue the soldiers of the BEF. The feared-for disaster was beginning to look increasingly like a success.

Ramsay, consequently, felt able to reduce the number of destroyers involved in *Dynamo*. In the course of the two previous days, eleven destroyers had been either sunk, disabled or damaged, leaving Dover Command with only seven modern destroyers to defend the Channel. With the agreement of the Admiralty, Ramsay withdrew these destroyers, leaving fifteen to continue with the evacuation. Even with this reduced capacity, Ramsay calculated that he could still maintain a rate of one destroyer per hour reaching Dunkirk – which meant these ships alone would be able to lift 17,000 men every twenty-four hours.

With these considerations in mind, Ramsay spelt out his arrangements for the night of 29/30 May in a signal to Tennant: 'Evacuation of British troops to continue at maximum speed during the night. If adequate supply of personnel vessels cannot be maintained to Dunkirk east pier [Mole], destroyers will be sent there as well. All other craft except hospital carriers to embark from beach which is extended from one mile east of Dunkirk to one mile east of La Panne. Whole length is divided into 3 equal parts referred to as La Panne, Bray, Malo, from east to west with a mile gap between each part. La Panne and Bray have troop concentration points each end and in the middle; Malo at each end. These points should be tended by inshore craft.'

Tennant was told to pass this information verbally on to those vessels not equipped with radio. However, Captain Tennant would not have to bear that responsibility alone, as shortly before midnight Rear Admiral Wake-Walker arrived in the destroyer HMS *Esk*. From that night onwards, Wake-Walker would be the Senior Naval Officer afloat, directing the ships from a motor boat, while Tennant directed operations on the shore. ✠

NOTES:
1. Quoted on the BBC History Archive, 'Voices of Dunkirk'.
2. IWM Sound Archive, Catalogue No.16722.
3. This tale is drawn from David Knowles, p.71.
4. Norman Wickman, 'A Royal Engineer at Dunkirk Tells His Story', *Warfare History Network*, 2 September 2016.
5. TNA WO 361/19.
6. TNA WO 361/19.
7. Gardner, p.46.

The graves of French and British troops, possibly killed during the loss of *Crested Eagle*, are examined by German troops after the evacuation. This is the stretch of beach where *Crested Eagle* was beached and wrecked, the paddle steamer being immediately out of view to the right.

AVIATION SPECIALS

RAF BATTLE OF BRITAIN MEMORIAL FLIGHT
Spectacularly celebrates the Flight's activities and achievements.

£5.99 inc FREE P&P*

SCALE MODELLING - MOSQUITO
Celebrates with five full model builds, type histories, kit/decal/accessory listings and exclusive scale drawings.

£5.99 inc FREE P&P*

SPITFIRE 80
Tribute to Britain's greatest fighter and possibly the best known combat aircraft in the world.

£5.99 inc FREE P&P*

VULCAN
A tribute to the most challenging and complex return-to-flight project ever.

£3.99 inc FREE P&P*

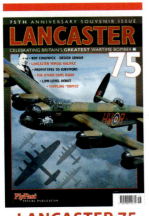

LANCASTER 75
Pays tribute to all who built, maintained and flew Lancasters, past and present.

£5.99 inc FREE P&P*

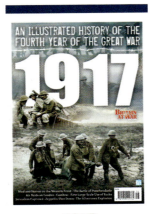

1917
An illustrated history of the fourth year of the great war.

£5.99 inc FREE P&P*

GULF WAR
A must-have for those seeking to understand the conflict that changed the shape of warfare.

£3.99 inc FREE P&P*

RAF OFFICIAL ANNUAL REVIEW 2017
Behind the scenes insight into the aircraft, equipment and people of one of the world's premier air forces.

£5.99 inc FREE P&P*

AVIATION SPECIALS

ESSENTIAL reading from the teams behind your **FAVOURITE** magazines

HOW TO ORDER

 OR

PHONE
UK: 01780 480404
ROW: (+44)1780 480404

*Prices correct at time of going to press. Free 2nd class P&P on all UK & BFPO orders. Overseas charges apply. Postage charges vary depending on total order value.

FREE Aviation Specials App

Simply download to purchase digital versions of your favourite aviation specials in one handy place! Once you have the app, you will be able to download new, out of print or archive specials for less than the cover price!

IN APP ISSUES **£3.99**

As dawn broke on 30 May, Rear Admiral Wake-Walker was able to see the magnitude of the task that confronted him. Along the beaches, long dark lines of men stretched to the water's edge and larger groups of men were gathered on the sands. He could also see the effects of the German bombing – *Bideford* aground with her stern blown off and the burnt-out remains of *Crested Eagle*.

Lying off the beaches were destroyers and other vessels to which men were making their way in small craft. A light swell made beach work difficult and many boats lay stranded by the tide. The troops, orderly and under control, continued to file down from the dunes, but the need,

still, was for boats and more boats. Part of the problem was that quite often, once the troops had climbed on board the ships, they just left the boats to float away on the tide as there were few naval ratings to act as boat-keepers.

It is surprising, therefore, that it was not until 13.15 hours on 30 May, that the War Ministry made contact with an obvious source of suitable vessels – the Royal National Lifeboat Institute. A phone call was made to the RNLI asking it to send as many of its boats as possible to Dover at once. That was all that was said and the instruction was not queried, though the reason for the call was easily guessed.[1]

As soon as the Institute received the call, it telephoned the eighteen stations around the south and east coasts within practicable

sailing distance of Dover, from Gorleston in Norfolk, which is 110 miles north-east of Dover, to Shoreham Harbour in Sussex, eighty miles to the west.

The lifeboat coxswains were ordered to make their way to Dover immediately for special duty with the Admiralty. They were told to take a full crew, full fuel-tanks and towing ropes. The first boats arrived at Dover that evening and another three reached the port early the next day. Within twenty-nine hours of the summons all bar three of the lifeboats had reached Dover. The lifeboats were going to war.

When the first of the lifeboat-men to arrive at Dover were told that they would be taking men off the beaches of Dunkirk, three of the crews, which manned heavy

DAY 5: 30 MAY

BELOW: **Abandoned Allied vehicles, including at least two Universal Carriers, at the top of the beach at Malo-les-Bains, to the east of Dunkirk, towards the end of Operation *Dynamo*. Note the harbour arm or East Mole that can be seen in the background.**
(All images Historic Military Press unless stated otherwise)

At last the 'Little Ships' were starting to arrive at Dunkirk in large numbers and evacuation from the beaches surpassed that from the harbour and the Mole.

An abandoned artillery piece on the promenade at Malo-les-Bains. In the background is the wreck of the French destroyer *L'Adroit*, which was sunk by Heinkel He 111 bombers in shallow water off Malo-les-Bains at 12.00 hours on 21 May 1940.

boats with deep keels that would have to be winched off the beaches, declined to go. Their boats were therefore taken over by the Royal Navy. The following lifeboat crews to arrive were given their course for Dunkirk and ordered into Dover for re-fuelling before their departure. They had not refused to go across the Channel but the Navy, worried about the morale of lifeboat-men after the refusal of the first three crews, decided to seize the boats and man them with their own officers and men. The brave, volunteer, lifeboat-men were very upset at this slight upon their honour, especially as some had anticipated being called into war service and had turned up at Dover with borrowed steel helmets.

However, two of the lifeboats were already at sea heading, not for Dover, but straight for Dunkirk and manned not by the Royal Navy but by the lifeboat crews themselves.

Earlier that morning, the naval officers-in-charge at Ramsgate and Margate had asked their lifeboats if they would sail for Dunkirk. Both crews agreed and, at 14.20 hours, *Prudential* left Ramsgate and a little more than three hours later *Lord Southborough* departed from Margate.

The eight-man crew of *Prudential*, under the command of Coxswain Howard Primrose Knight, was issued with gas masks and steel helmets and cans of fresh water for the soldiers that they would be saving from the beaches of Dunkirk. Coxswain Knight

was also given four coils of grass warp rope. This particular type of rope is made from coconut fibre. It is not as strong as manila but it is much lighter and floats in the water. The advantage of this is that, when towing, there is far less chance of the rope becoming entangled in the boats' propellers. It is interesting to note that one of the things that delayed the transport of some of the Little Ships was a shortage of hawsers in and around the south coast ports and appeals were made to other ports further north to send what they could.

Prudential took in tow eight boats manned by eighteen men from the Royal Navy. Most of these boats were wherrys, a type of simple, light rowing-boat. It would be the task of ▶

Two further views of the wreck of *L'Adroit* at Malo-les-Bains. Despite frequently appearing in pictures relating to Operation *Dynamo*, her loss predates the official start of the evacuation.

the Ramsgate lifeboat to tow the wherrys between the beaches and the ships standing out to sea. By contrast, *Lord Southborough* herself was towed across the Channel by a large Dutch barge commanded by a naval officer. Coxswain Edward Drake Parker's ten-man crew was also supplied with steel helmets and food and cigarettes. The scene that day was described by Ernest Long:

'I could see the masts of sunken ships all over the harbour. Some had been blasted onto the beach, and there was evidence of aircraft dogfights with parts of shot-down planes of both sides littering the sands. There were hastily prepared slit trenches dug by those who had preceded us and in quite a lot of these trenches were dead bodies of those who had

been killed by enemy action. It was a terrible gruesome sight.

'The harbour master and his assistants were trying desperately hard to organise the embarking troops into any boat or ship that had managed to reach the side of the Mole. When my turn came I remember having to balance across a gangplank that had been put across a part of the Mole that had received a direct hit. That hit had left a wide gap between the two sections.'[2]

Despite such difficulties, embarkation continued from the Mole, the ships having to manoeuvre round the growing number of wrecks.

WITHIN THE PERIMETER

The perimeter was, by 30 May, beginning to take on a solid form, running for twenty-five miles from the right of Nieuport to the town of Bergues, which was the only position held forward of the Bergues-Furnes canal and formed the limit of the British line, and then westwards along the French-held sector to Mardyck. I Corps held the western half of the British sector, from Dunkirk to the French frontier, whilst II Corps occupied the eastern part from the frontier to the sea at Nieuport. The weakest point of the perimeter was in the area of Dunkirk itself where III Corps' severely-mauled 44th and 48th divisions were in no state to mount a determined defence.

To help coordinate the evacuation, Captain J.M. Howson was appointed Naval-Officer-in-Charge of beaches. As the first light of day broke over Dunkirk, Howson had his first glimpse of the scene off Bray: 'In the lightening dawn, a number of destroyers, sloops and skoots were seen to be lying off, and embarkation was proceeding in such boats as were available. Several boats were aground, others holed, and some had no oars … By about 0600 all destroyers, sloops, etc., had cleared for England and there were no further ships available.' This demonstrated, of course, the need for more ships, but also that the embarkation was now being organised better and the ships being filled up more quickly.

The paddle steamer *Princess Elizabeth* was built in 1927 by Day Summers of Southampton for Red Funnel Steamers. Her first trip to Dunkirk began at 13.00 hours on 29 May when she sailed from Dover, arriving at La Panne at 20.13 hours. She left for Margate at 05.36 hours on the 30th with 450 troops on board. Having survived the war, *Princess Elizabeth* returned to Dunkirk for the last time in 1999, where she serves as a venue for city events and festivities. (Courtesy of Dunkirk Tourism)

An iconic image of soldiers under fire on the beaches at Dunkirk during the evacuation.

The beaches themselves, after four days of bombardment, presented a sorry spectacle as Sergeant A. Bruce of the 7th Field Company, Royal Engineers saw: 'As we trudged on, we passed horses, their stomachs ripped apart and entrails scattered all over the place. Men were lying there in grotesque attitude of death, eyes and mouths wide open; it was hard to believe that they had ever been human beings … here they lay where they had died, like dogs that had been run over in the street.'[3]

During the morning sappers and troops of the 1st Division built a long pier of lorries stretching into the sea at Bray and decked it with planks. This would help speed up the embarkation as at low tide even many

of the 'Little Ships', could not get close to the beaches. Around fifteen three-ton lorries were placed side by side on Bray-Dunes' hard sand during low tide. Bullets fired at their tyres punctured them and this, together with sand thrown into the backs of lorries and the fact that they were lashed together after the covers were stripped of their superstructure, ensured that they did not move when the tide came in. Decking panels from bridging trucks laid across the backs of lorries, along with planks 'liberated' from a local timber yard, served as the walkway along which soldiers could make their way out to the launches and boats that came to collect them.[4] This pier proved so successful that a similar one was built at La Panne (others soon followed).

Operating from Bray, Howson signalled to the arriving ships to go ashore as the pier offered additional opportunities for the ships to take men directly off the beach – and there were now more vessels available than on any previous day.

At Bray evacuation went better as more shipping arrived there and divisions which had waited patiently for many hours were taken off. Fifteen French vessels also arrived and entered Dunkirk – two destroyers, three torpedo boats, two minesweepers, four trawlers, a tug and three fishing vessels.[5]

Also during the morning Gort and Wake-Walker met to discuss the final phase of the evacuation. It was agreed that the last reasonable date at which the BEF might ➡

Although illustrative of events at Dunkirk in May and June 1940, this dramatic shot of soldiers wading out from a beach to a waiting small craft with rifles held high is taken from the 1958 film *Dunkirk*.

Visible to all those approaching Dunkirk by land, sea and air, and from some distance away, were the palls of black smoke towering over the port. They were caused by the oil tanks in the harbour area having been set alight to prevent their capture by the Germans. Note the 220 Squadron Lockheed Hudson in the foreground.

be expected to hold its part of the perimeter was daybreak on 1 June, with the army being reduced by that time to a rear-guard of just 4,000 men. Wake-Walker knew that by then he would have a large number of suitable boats at his disposal – ocean-going tugs and lifeboats – to bring off these last men in one lift. It was therefore agreed that Wake-Walker would ensure that he retained the necessary craft for this last lift which was to begin at 01.30 hours on 1 June. Hopefully, by the time it was light enough for the Germans to see the beach clearly, the BEF would have gone.

Heavy cloud and poor visibility made air operations very difficult during the 30th and it brought some respite from the German attacks. Fighter Command, on the other hand, patrolled at three- or four-squadron strength at frequent intervals throughout the day and the only enemy bombers they met were driven off. Bomber Command also played its part, with Blenheims attacking the German forces south of Dunkirk during the day and Wellingtons bombing the German columns heading for Dunkirk. Major L.F. Ellis, the official historian of the Second World War, described one of the successful examples of the RAF's operation which took place late in the evening. 'There had been fighting all day at Nieuport and while attack and counter-attack had led to no great change, the enemy was moving up additional troops and the threat of a real break-through was serious. In the early evening six Albacores of the Fleet Air Arm and eighteen Blenheims bombed the enemy in Nieuport and troops behind the town massing for a further attack. The enemy's concentration there was broken up and no further attack was made before the 4th Division retired to the beaches.'[6]

The rate of embarkation was increasing, helped by the arrival of what Ramsay called 'freelance' boats. As well as helping to take men directly off the beaches, they also recovered many of the small boats that had been abandoned and drifted out to sea. These small boats, of all kinds, were arriving in convoy after convoy. These included five little craft, *Bee*, *Bat*, *Chamois*, *Hound* and *M.F.H.*, from the removal firm Pickfords – they were vessels built to carry items between the mainland and the Isle of Wight. Three of these were manned by their own civilian crews. *Chamois* came under air attack and was twice forced to pull back. When she made a third attempt, she got to within two miles of Dunkirk but went to the help of two ships that had been bombed and were on fire. This twenty-five-metre-long steel barge with its two-man crew, of E. Brown and L. Church, rescued 130 men from the burning ships, all of whom were French or Belgian.

Duncan Nicol, a former navy stoker, was assigned to *Elizabeth Green*, a small pleasure craft with a rowing boat attached. He helped row the little boat backwards and forwards taking as many men as it could carry to an anchored warship: 'We continued ferrying from the beach to the sloop, but on leaving the beach each time there was appeals to come back and on one occasion, when I said we have enough, we can't take any more, a little man, wearing glasses, a little soldier, he put his four fingers to hold the side of the whaler, and he said, "will you please take me because I don't think I can stand any more. I shall be dead before you get back." There was a sergeant in the whaler and he crashed his rifle down on this man's fingers and said, "You heard what the man said and we can't take any more", and he completely severed the four fingers which fell into the bottom of the boat. The little man just fell back into the water and presumably died.'[7]

The flow of troops through the perimeter had also improved, with less men crowding onto the beaches. The intense bombing of the previous day had also resulted in the order being given that on the 30th only one destroyer at a time should berth against

The dense black smoke rising into the sky over Dunkirk as seen from the land. This picture was actually taken by a German soldier during the enemy advance.

Burning oil tanks as seen from patrolling RAF aircraft.

The collapsed and badly damaged oil tanks pictured after the end of Operation *Dynamo*.

The wreck of the paddle steamer *Devonia* on the beach at La Panne, where it was deliberately beached after being damaged in an air raid on 30 May 1940. *Devonia* had made several journeys to and from the beaches before it was abandoned.

BELOW RIGHT: **One RNLI lifeboat to serve during *Dynamo* was Aldeburgh's** *Lucy Lavers*. **Commanded during the operation by Sub-Lieutenant T. Betts RNVR,** *Lucy Lavers* **survived the war – this picture being taken in Wells Harbour.** (Courtesy of Chris Holifield; www.geograph.org.uk)

the East Mole. But the reduced effort by the Luftwaffe on the 30th because of the poor weather encouraged Commander Guy Maund RN (who was temporary SNO whilst Tennant was in conference at La Panne with Lord Gort to discuss the arrangements for the final evacuation) to try to improve the rate of embarkation still further by, at 17.00 hours, instructing ships waiting off shore to use the Mole if they could find berthing space.

The Luftwaffe was not completely idle, though, and it delivered repeated attacks, many of the aircraft targeting not the ships loading troops, but the already-wrecked vessels. 'We got a great deal of amusement and satisfaction from this, for loading was proceeding apace with no casualties', as Maund later reported: 'I decided that the rate of embarkation must in some way be speeded up as the capacity of the ships now alongside was more than adequate for the rate of the

flow of troops. This laid our vessels open to attack from the air … I therefore went down to the Eastern Arm [Mole] and rigged up a loud speaker [which had been sent over on the 30th] and addressed the troops in the following terms: "Remember your pals, boys. The quicker you get on board, the more of them will be saved."

'This worked like a miracle. The thousands of troops, tired, depressed, and without food or water for days, broke into a double and kept it up for the whole length of the Eastern Arm for more than two hours.'[8]

Maund's encouragement certainly paid dividends as around 15,000 men were taken off the East Mole between 18.00 hours and 21.00 hours.

During that time, apart from other ships using the East Mole, eight destroyers rescued 8,528 and the vessels *Prague*, *Royal Sovereign*, *St Helier* and *Tynwald* recovered 5,694 troops. A hospital carrier, which berthed at the far end of the Mole, also took a number of wounded on board.

French ships also began to arrive on the 30th. Some fifteen vessels reached Dunkirk harbour, including the destroyers *Foudroyant* and *Branlebas* and the torpedo boats *Bourrasque*, *Bouclier* and *Siroco*. *Bourrasque*'s participation in Operation *Dynamo* did not last long, however.

She left Dunkirk at 15.30 hours from the Quai Félix Faure with more than 600 men (and one woman). Around thirty minutes later, as she was passing Nieuport, she came under fire from a German battery. The French boat moved as far over as she could to the edge of the swept channel but when the torpedo boat was about five miles north of Nieuport she was shaken by a violent explosion, followed by a second even-more violent one. The ship came to a halt, badly damaged.

Understandably, there was a degree of panic amongst the passengers, who believed the ship was sinking. Even though the captain had not declared that the warship should be abandoned, the ship's boats were lowered but so many crowded into them that they sank. Others jumped into the water. *Bourrasque* was indeed sinking, having ▶

A pre-war picture of the paddle steamer *Devonia*.

Wrecked ships, vehicles and other debris on the beach at Dunkirk. In the right foreground is the wreck of the skoot *Sursum Corda* which ran aground on its third trip ferrying troops between the beach at Malo-les-Bains and the larger vessels offshore. Requisitioned at Poole, where it had been lying at the start of *Dynamo*, *Sursum Corda*, commanded by Lieutenant C. Philpotts RN, is recorded as having rescued 370 men.

either struck a mine or been hit by artillery, sources disagree on this point, and broke in two. The destroyer *Branlebas*, with 300 troops on board, was astern of *Bourrasque* and picked up 100 survivors. The Admiralty drifter *Yorkshire Lass*, and the armed trawler HMT *Ut Prosim* also helped. Remarkably, at 05.30 hours on the 31st, the Pickfords' boat *Bat* picked up another fifteen survivors from the partially submerged wreck. They were found completely naked and covered in oil.

THE LIFEBOATS ARRIVE

The lifeboat *Prudential* reached Dunkirk at 20.00 hours. A light westerly wind was blowing and a dense black cloud of smoke from the burning oil-tanks swirled around and above the shore and the sea. Above the smoke, wave after wave of Stukas and Messerschmitts bombed and gunned the helpless troops on the beaches and in the water. Howard Knight moved *Prudential* two miles along the coast to Malo-les-Bains to lay alongside a Dutch coaster until it was dark.

With the fall of night, Coxswain Knight sent three of his wherrys to the shore each with one of his lifeboat-men on board. They rowed carefully towards the land shouting into the dark until they heard an answering call. Locating the desperate soldiers, the boats filled up with men. Knight then sent three more boats with twelve of the naval men. The sailors were to man the oars of the six boats and push the boats off the beach. The three boats set off but never returned.

So Knight sent a seventh boat with three sailors and, along with the other three boats, ferried increasing numbers of troops back to *Prudential*. It was a slow and difficult

The Eastbourne lifeboat *Jane Holland* was the oldest of the RNLI fleet at Dunkirk. She was also the one to survive the greatest damage. Taken across the Channel by a naval crew on 30 May, she immediately set about ferrying troops. But things did not go well, and she was soon in trouble. A French motor torpedo boat had hit her forward in the confused melee inshore and, while the crew struggled to repair the damage, she was hit again. This time it was aft, and by a Royal Navy motor torpedo boat! She struggled on until, about half a mile offshore, the engine failed – a point at which *Jane Holland* came under heavy fire from German artillery onshore. She was also attacked by German aircraft. The crew finally 'abandoned ship' and were rescued by a passing boat. A French destroyer, considering her to be a hazard, attempted to sink her with gunfire. As a result of all this attention, *Jane Holland* was reported as lost, only to be found a few days later drifting, abandoned, in the Channel. The damage was extensive – her bows had been riddled by more than 500 machine-gun bullets, the fore-end box was badly stove in, and she was heavily water-logged. Incredibly, *Jane Holland* was repaired, returned to Eastbourne and continued to serve the RNLI until 1949.

operation. Each boat was rowed in stern first. The sailors would grab the rocking boat and hold it steady in the rolling surf until the troops waded out. There was no rush or panic. The soldiers only moved forward, waist-high in the water, when their officers gave the word. Just one man at a time could climb over the stern and a full boat amounted to a mere eight men.

Prudential could hold 160 men fully-laden and eventually she reached capacity and Knight had to transfer the troops to a ship that lay further out in the deeper water. Back to her post went the Ramsgate lifeboat and by daybreak she had taken some 800 men off the Dunkirk beaches.

The wreck of *Devonia* as it appears today on the beach near Bray-les-Dunes. The remains lie a short distance from those of *Crested Eagle*. (Courtesy of Christophe Bonte)

German soldiers 'guard' *Devonia*'s wreck in the aftermath of Operation *Dynamo*. The wreck was broken up in situ during 1941.

Looking from the remains of *Devonia* out over the beach at Bray towards the sand dunes.

On one of its trips to the shore during the night a voice called out to *Prudential*, 'I cannot see who you are. Are you a naval party?' 'No, sir', replied one of the lifeboat-men, 'we are the men of the crew of the Ramsgate lifeboat'. The voice called back, 'Thank you, and thank God for such men as you have this night proved yourselves to be.'[9]

Nightfall also saw a renewed attempt by the Germans to cross the canal at and just north of the small town of Furnes. Earlier, the Germans had launched their most determined effort of the day against this section of the perimeter which was held by the 7th Guards Brigade and the 8th Brigade. The attack was beaten off, but the 4th Battalion, Royal Berkshire Regiment was so severely depleted in numbers that a company of the 1st Coldstream Guards was sent to take over that part of the line.

Harry Dennis of the 1st Battalion, East Surrey Regiment, had been ordered to take a message to the Berkshires: 'I eventually found them. They looked as though they had been put through a mincer. I approached a young officer. "I'm looking for the Commanding Officer of the Berkshires," I said. "That's me," he replied. He was a Lieutenant, not a Colonel or Major or Captain. It appeared they were down to 87 men in the battalion.'[10]

Furnes itself was held by the 1st and 2nd battalions, Grenadier Guards. Signalman

George Jones was with the 1st Battalion: 'We saw and felt the town of Furnes tumble about us. The Germans expended untold quantities of ammunition upon the area, and us! Driven into the depths of cellars, rows of red bricked houses became an inferno of exploding rooftops.'[11]

At around 22.00 hours the attack was renewed and the enemy succeeded in breaking across the canal. But the Guards counter-attacked, drove them back across the water and restored the front.[12]

By the end of Day 5 of Operation *Dynamo* 53,823 men had been rescued, of whom 29,512 had been taken off the beaches and 24,311 from the harbour and the East Mole. The total recovered for these five days was 126,606. According to Gort's estimation, there remained just 80,000 British troops within the perimeter. His job was all but done. This was made clear to him in a message from the Secretary of State:

'Continue to defend the present perimeter to the utmost in order to cover maximum evacuation now proceeding well. Report every three hours through La Panne. If we can still communicate we shall send you an order to return to England with such officers as you may choose at the moment when we deem your command so reduced that it can be handed over to a Corps Commander. If communications are broken you are to hand over and return as specified when

your effective fighting force does not exceed the equivalent of three divisions. This is in accordance with correct military procedure and no personal discretion is left to you in the matter.

'On political grounds, it would be a needless triumph to the enemy to capture you when only a small force remained under your orders. The Corps Commander chosen by you should be ordered to carry on the defence in conjunction with the French and evacuated whether from Dunkirk or the beaches, but when in his judgement no further proportionate damage can be inflicted on the enemy he is authorised in consultation with the senior French Commander to capitulate formally to avoid useless slaughter.'

Gort had been sent to defend the great nation of France and had found himself defending just a few square miles by the sea. Though he had been forced to withdraw, there was no ignominy in the retreat to Dunkirk. The BEF had not been defeated, and now he could hand over command in the knowledge that the bulk of the army was already safely back in the UK, and would be able to fight another day.[13] ✚

NOTES:
1. Martin Mace, *They Also Served: The Story of Sussex Lifeboats at War 1939-1945* (Historic Military Press, Storrington, 2001), pp.7-8.
2. Quoted in Patrick Wilson, pp.148-9.
3. Quoted in Robert Jackson, *Dunkirk, The British Evacuation* (Arthur Baker, London, 1976), p.117.
4. Cited in Hugh Sebag-Montefiore: *Dunkirk: Fight to the Last Man* (Penguin, London, 2006) p.415.
5. L.F. Ellis, *The War in France and Flanders 1939-1940* (HMSO, London, 1954), p.232.
6. ibid, p.235.
7. *Yesterday's Witness, One Man's Dunkirk*, BBC Archive.
8. Captain Maund's report, quoted in Gardner, pp.63-4.
9. C. Vince, *Storm on the Waters: The Story of the Life-Boat Service in the War of 1939-1945* (Hodder & Stoughton, London 1946), p.29.
10. Quoted, unsourced, in Patrick Wilson, *Dunkirk, From Disaster to Deliverance* (Leo Cooper, Barnsley, 1999), pp.102-3.
11. ibid, pp.104-5.
12. Ellis, p.226.
13. ibid, p.230.

A pre-war image of the lifeboat *Edward Z. Dresden* which, based at Clacton-on-Sea, was one of the nineteen RNLI vessels that participated in the Dunkirk evacuation.

DAY 6:31 MAY

Against all expectations, the Germans had failed to prevent the evacuation of the BEF but there were still tens of thousands of men waiting on the exposed beaches.

It had been thought that the evacuation would only last for forty-eight hours before it was terminated by enemy action but after five days the perimeter still held, despite repeated attempts by the Germans to cross the Furnes-Bergues canal in rubber boats throughout the 30th. The Germans, therefore, concentrated their efforts on the town of Furnes, held by the 1st and 2nd battalions, Grenadier Guards during the night of 30/31 May. It seemed evident that this part of the perimeter could not hold much longer and if the enemy could break through at this point they could swoop down on La Panne, and the tired and almost defenceless troops would be slaughtered.

TOP RIGHT: **A heavily loaded destroyer edges its way into Dover to disembark its cargo of Allied troops.** (Courtesy of Pen & Sword Books)

MAIN PICTURE: **French and British troops on board ships berthing at Dover, 31 May 1940.** (All images Historic Military Press unless stated otherwise)

The whole of the German operations against Dunkirk were finally put under a single command – that of General Georg von Küchler's Eighteenth Army of Army Group B – the change taking place at 02.00 hours on the 31st. This was to release Rundstedt's panzer divisions for the drive south towards the Somme, where it was believed that a large French army was still intact.

The Battle of France was still not won and, as had already been seen, it was the panzer divisions which were the most effective, and already Rundstedt had lost nearly half of his armoured strength. To waste any more of his tanks in the broken, ditch-strewn fields around Dunkirk against an enemy that no longer posed a threat and was evacuating would have been a poor use of such a resource. So, the Eighteenth Army, which had been engaged in Holland and against the Belgian Army, was now made responsible for the destruction or capture of the Allied troops in the bridgehead. The forces which came under von Küchler's command were the IX, X, XIV and XXVI Corps, which included the Leibstandarte *SS Adolf Hitler*.[1]

As a result of these changes, heavy shelling of the beaches by the German artillery during the night had ceased by 03.00 hours, allowing large numbers of troops to be evacuated and by dawn the beaches were very nearly clear of troops. The following extract from the report of Captain Howson, S.N.O. on the beaches, illustrates conditions at Bray at this time:

'At 0400 there was a very considerable number of destroyers, paddlers, trawlers, skoots, etc., off Bray, and embarkation was proceeding satisfactorily, but a lop [choppy sea conditions] had already started. There were about 10 motor yachts which had arrived from England. These craft drew 6-7 feet and were unable to get close in to any of the beaches.

'During the forenoon, considerable towing of empty craft towards the beach was carried out, and only about two boats were allowed to get adrift and ultimately ground. With the falling tide, however, a number of boats were seen to ground and remain ashore

until the tide rose in the afternoon … Other power boats broke down. Nevertheless, the embarkation, much hindered by the lop, proceeded satisfactorily. As further destroyers and sloops arrived, they were directed to lower their motor boats and whalers as this had not already been done; these boats were quite invaluable. About noon, the lop began to subside and with the rising tide conditions for embarkation very greatly improved, more boats were sent in and more boats floated off and matters were proceeding very well.' ▶

Massey Shaw in action off Dunkirk during the evacuation. Note the smoke from the burning oil tanks in the background.

It was not only Allied personnel who were evacuated from Dunkirk. Here a group of German prisoners of war, complete with identifying patches on their backs, are escorted onto one of the evacuation ships for the journey to a camp in Britain.

The respite from the shelling did not last long and it was still early morning when German artillery near Nieuport opened-up and began shelling the shore at La Panne with great accuracy. A number of the small boats were sunk and the embarkation was disrupted as the ships moved westwards out of range of the enemy guns.

The Eighteenth Army launched a major assault upon the perimeter held by II Corps. The 4th Battalion, East Yorkshire Regiment and the 4th and 5th battalions, the Green Howards of 150th Brigade, found themselves in an almost indefensible position, as the Officer Commanding 'C' Company, 5th Battalion Green Howards, Captain Tony Steele, was all too painfully aware:

'My Company had a frontage of 800 yards, which was far too big to hold successfully. More important still, the German side of the canal in front of us was completely wooded, whereas on the Dunkirk side the terrain was completely flat and open. We dug in in sections and there was absolutely no way to camouflage the trenches; the enemy just climbed trees on the other side, spotted every last one of our positions on the ground

that was as flat as your hand, then brought up their heavy mortars and systematically plastered us.'[2]

The 1/6th Battalion, East Surrey Regiment of the 10th Brigade also came under heavy pressure, the Germans crossing the canal at first light and storming the brickworks it held as a strongpoint. The East Surrey's 1st Battalion from the 11th Brigade was sent to help. The perimeter held, but only just. At one stage the two battalion commanders had to man a Bren gun together, with one lieutenant colonel feeding the gun while the other fired it.[3]

There was an even closer call when a massive assault upon the 8th Brigade saw the Germans break through the perimeter near Furnes. The 2nd Battalion Grenadier Guards was sent to plug the gap. Second Lieutenant Jones found two battalions of the brigade in a state of panic, abandoning their positions. The fate of the BEF hung in the balance. The men had been spooked and nothing, it seemed, could stop them running away – until they faced the bayonets of the Grenadiers. Jones managed to restore order, even being

forced to shoot some of the panicked troops. The line held and by the middle of the afternoon the enemy pulled back.[4]

The Germans, though, were far from finished. The Durham Light Infantry, its 6th, 8th and 9th battalions, forming II Corps' 151st Brigade, held the small village of Les Moeres ten kilometres north-east of Bergues. Again, the Germans stormed across the canal, and again the line held. The Germans then did what they should have done before their attack and bombarded the DLI's positions. The German shells hammered into the main building in the village, the château, which the DLI had to abandon.

Furnes, held by the 1st Battalion Grenadier Guards, also came under attack, as did the positions along the canal to the east of the town where the 2nd Battalion Coldstream Guards were posted. These battalions of I Corps held their ground until nightfall when

The River Thames fire float *Massey Shaw* berthed in London's Surrey Quays. One of the 'Little Ships', she can be seen in the 1958 film *Dunkirk* starring John Mills and Richard Attenborough. (Courtesy of Bill Scott)

Members of the crew of *Massey Shaw* parade through London in the aftermath of their involvement in Operation *Dynamo*.

The Maritime Hospital at Zuydcoote was badly damaged during the evacuation, and buildings within its grounds, and well as those in the immediate vicinity (such as that seen here on the main drive to the hospital), still bear the scars of the fighting in the area during May and June 1940.

the decision to thin the line came into effect and the Grenadiers were told to make their way to the beach. From 1 June onwards the perimeter would be occupied by far fewer troops and it would require heroic action to hold it. This would result in the award of a Victoria Cross, the story of which will soon be told.

MORE LITTLE SHIPS

The morning had seen the loss of the French destroyer *Siroco* after being attacked by German E-boats. She was on her way to Dover with 770 troops from Dunkirk, when the noise of aircraft was heard overhead and the skipper slowed to seven knots to reduce her phosphorescent wake. Waiting silently in the dark were *S.23* and *S.26*. At 01.45 hours *Siroco* was hit by two torpedoes. A column of flame was seen to shoot 200 feet into the air. Moments later she rolled over and sank. Only 252 men survived.[5]

Vessels of all descriptions arrived throughout the 31st. A semi-official record of the services of many of the 'Little Ships' was compiled after Operation *Dynamo* by one of the Naval officers that travelled with the first flotilla, Temporary Lieutenant A. Dann. In this, Dann portrays the assembly of these vessels with eloquence:

'From all around the compass they came. From up the river, along the coast, from the yachting harbours, the pleasure beaches, Naval ports and fishing towns – anything that would float, move under its own power, or collect a dozen or so men from the beaches where they waited. Each boat with its own tiny crew was thrown more or less upon its own resources; and upon the fortunes of war and the initiative of each boat's captain depends the story each may subsequently tell.'[6]

These included cockle boats from the Thames Estuary which had never ventured beyond those waters and only one of the crews had ventured further than Ramsgate. Six of these came from Leigh-on-Sea – *Renown*, *Reliant*, *Endeavour*, *Leticia*, *Resolute* and *Defender*. When they arrived off the beaches of Bray and La Panne, it was found that the swell was too great for the small boats to try and take men off the beaches. Instead, they operated a form of ferry service, taking troops off the East Mole to the larger ships waiting in deeper water.

On board *Leticia* was 'Jimmy' Dench: 'During the penultimate ferrying trip from the small fishing boats to the larger ships out at sea: a shell burst between the last boat and us. We turned back to go out, but the signaler that we had on board, and who had only

been "out" for about six weeks and never been under fire, said, "We've got to go in again" (to rescue more soldiers). So we went in.'

Over the course of eight hours, as the evacuation was reaching its conclusion, these boats helped rescue hundreds of troops as the Germans closed in upon the Dunkirk perimeter. When there was no more that they could do, the Essex fishermen headed back to England – but then tragedy struck. Jimmy Dench described the incident: 'We saw another boat coming up behind us. It was the *Renown*, and, yelling that they had engine trouble, they made fast to our stern … We towed them 3.5 fathoms of rope being the distance between us. That was 1.15 am [1 June] … Tired out, the engineer, seaman and signaller went to turn in, when, at about 1.50 am, a terrible explosion took place, and hail of wood splinters came down on our deck. In the pitch dark, you could see nothing, and we could do nothing … except pull the tow rope which was just as we passed it to the *Renown* about three quarters of an hour before.'

Renown had hit a mine and the little fishing boat and all three fishermen from Leigh-on-Sea that were on board were blown to pieces, along with a young seaman from the Merchant Navy who had volunteered to join the crew.[7] Ramsay wrote of these men that: ⊳

Allied troops wade out into the water near the imposing Maritime Hospital at Zuydcoote, near Bray Dunes, to the east of Dunkirk.

Two views of a large party of troops disembarking from a destroyer at Dover, 31 May 1940. One soldier is carrying a ceremonial sword, presumably a 'souvenir' of the campaign.

'They were all volunteers who were rushed over to Dunkirk in one day, probably none of them had been under gunfire before and certainly not under Naval discipline … In spite of this … all orders were carried out with great diligence even under actual shell fire and aircraft attack.'[8]

Henry John Osborne was hoping to gain a commission with the RNVR and was actually attending a lecture on 30 May, for a qualification in 'practical piloting' that would help his application, when the lecture was interrupted. The attendees asked to report to the Port of London Authority Building near the Tower of London at 18.30 hours that evening. They were told to man lifeboats that had been taken from sea-going ships. These were then formed in lines of four or five boats and towed over to Dunkirk by tug. Henry takes up his story after they had reached the beaches:

'The troops were very well disciplined, just waiting in long columns, hoping to be taken off. They were all dead beat, having had a terrible time fighting their way to the beaches. We were able to get right to the sandy beach and took on board about 30 British soldiers. They were travelling "light" having discarded most of their equipment. We rowed away from the shore and took our "passengers" to the nearest craft lying off shore that we could find, a tug, a drifter, a trawler, anything that could risk coming in so close.

'We returned to the beach; probably a different section because as soon as we approached a crowd of French soldiers, with all their equipment, rushed out into the water and climbed on board before we had a chance to turn the boat around headed out to sea. As the tide was falling we became stuck on the sand. With great difficulty, we persuaded the Frenchman to get out of the boat and we were then able to turn it round and prevent it broaching (getting broadside onto the sea).

'At one time, I was almost up to my neck in the water holding the bow of the boat pointed out to seawards – still in my "interview" suit! We transferred that load eventually to one of the waiting craft and made one or two more trips before deciding dawn was approaching and it was our turn to make the return journey and get on the way before daylight.

Looking down the length of one of at least two piers constructed on the beach at La Panne, it being the 'Kursaal' building that can be seen on the right in the background. According to one account, Lieutenant Harold Dibbens RMP was responsible for one of the piers on this stretch of coast. His company, 102 Provost, 'drove the lorries onto the beach and they were held together and modified into a jetty by a group of some 30 Royal Engineers under the command of Captain E.H. Sykes. They tied the lorries together, slashed tyres and weighed them down with sandbags and heavy objects to stop them moving when the tide came in. Planks of wood were lashed to the roofs of the lorries to enable soldiers to walk out to the waiting boats.'

A view of abandoned Allied vehicles on the beach in front of the Malo Terminus Casino after the end of Operation *Dynamo*.

BOTTOM MIDDLE: **Evacuated members of the BEF pictured soon after their arrival back in the UK.**

'Through all this time we were so occupied with what we were doing that we were hardly aware of all the other activity going on all around us. It is always like this "in action". There were aircraft overhead, friend and foe, all the time; continual bombardment of the town, harbour and of the beaches by the Germans. Ships were being sunk and survivors rescued. All around the town and harbour of Dunkirk fires were blazing, a heavy pall of smoke hanging over it all. From much further off shore the British ships were bombarding the German positions.

'We eventually left the beaches just before dawn on Saturday, 1st June.'[9]

As seems to be the case, quite the opposite from the ordered, controlled embarkation was experienced by others, including Coxswain Parker of the Margate lifeboat *Lord Southborough*:

'There was a nasty surf. Troops were rushing out to get to us from all directions and were being drowned close to us and we could not get to them … it seemed to me we were doing more harm [than good] by drawing the men off the shore, as with their heavy clothing, the surf was knocking them over and they were unable to get up.'[10]

The swell, caused by a stiffening on-shore breeze, was indeed making things very difficult. Many of the towing-boats had capsized and had lost their crews, and the motor boats were being tossed around so much in the surf that they could not reach the beach. So work began on an improvised

pier at La Panne which, it was hoped, would be beyond the range of the German artillery at Nieuport.

Nowhere though, was beyond the range of the Luftwaffe, and once the early morning haze had burnt off enemy aircraft mounted three raids during the day, at 14.15 hours, 17.00 hours and 19.00 hours. Fighter Command did what it could, flying eight patrols with 289 Spitfires, Hurricanes and Defiants in large multi-squadron sorties. It proved to be a bad day for the RAF, losing nineteen aircraft whilst only able to claim ten enemy machines.

To help control the troops on the beaches, a contingent of twelve Royal Navy and sixty ratings was sent across the Channel late on the evening of the 29th. Having split into parties of one officer, one petty officer, one leading seaman, two able seamen, and one signaller, these teams began work in the early hours of the 30th, continuing their task well in the following day. One of those officers, Lieutenant J.G. Wells, having been assigned a stretch of beach at Bray, saw that the troops were, 'eager to get off the beach at any cost. Some had been waiting for forty-eight hours and all had witnessed the bombing that day by German aircraft.'

Wells later described how the evacuation was then arranged: 'The system that produced the best results, was to organise them into a long queue at each of the three embarkation points at Bray beach. The queues were three deep and were spaced out in groups of ten this number being most suitable for the types of boat available. The following group could be used for shoving off a loaded boat, which took a good deal of moving at half-tide owing to a bar running parallel to the sea.'

With insufficient naval ratings to man the boats, they were simply abandoned by the soldiers, and the sailors often had to swim out to recover the empty boats. Nevertheless, Lieutenant Wells was complimentary about the conduct of the troops: 'Their behaviour under shell fire … was a fine example to the ▶

German troops in the bomb and shell damaged streets of the town of Bergues during their final advance on Dunkirk.

RIGHT: **Evacuated soldiers disembarking at Dover. Though tired and weary, these men have nonetheless reached the safety of British soil.**

Destroyers loaded with soldiers evacuated from Dunkirk pictured after their return to Dover, this being an image believed to have been taken on 31 May 1940. The warship in the background with the pennant number D-94 is the destroyer HMS *Whitehall*.

sailors, who soon picked up the idea of lying flat on the stomach and singing "Roll out the barrel".'

SHARING THE EVACUATION WITH THE FRENCH

One of the more unusual boats to reach the evacuation beaches was the River Thames fire float *Massey Shaw*. Whilst there was some suggestion that she might be able to put out some of the fires raging in Dunkirk harbour, it was *Massey Shaw*'s shallow draft, of less than four feet, that was of the greatest appeal to the Admiralty. She set off on 30 May with a volunteer crew of thirteen under Sub-Officer A. J. May. The fire float was never expected to leave the calm waters of the Thames; it would be a rocky ride across the Channel.

Having picked up a naval lieutenant, and a chart, at Ramsgate, *Massey Shaw* arrived off Bray-Dunes on the afternoon of the 31st. She moved close into the shore, sending a light skiff, picked up at Ramsgate, to one of the many queues that had formed along the beach. The moment the boat was close enough, the troops at the head of the column rushed onto the boat which promptly sank. The crew then saw a stranded RAF speedboat which they salvaged and sent to the beach, only for the scene to be repeated and the speedboat went down under a mass of desperate soldiers.

It was not until 23.00 hours that another boat was found, by which time the crew of *Massey Shaw* had worked out a solution to the problem. A line was run from the fire float to an abandoned lorry on the beach and the new boat was pulled along this rope like, as one historian described it, a 'sea-going trolley car'.[11] The little boat could only carry six men at a time, but forwards and backwards it travelled until she was full, having taken on board forty men of a company of Royal Engineers. *Massey Shaw* made her way back to Ramsgate during the night, surviving an attack from a German bomber which had spotted its phosphorescent wake.

The evacuation, though, was going much better than expected and Churchill decided

that the French troops should be given an equal opportunity of being evacuated in British ships and boats. This was relayed to Alexander, by the Secretary of State, Eden, at 20.15 hours: 'You should withdraw your force as rapidly as possible on a 50-50 basis with the French Army, aiming at completion by night of 1-2 June. You should inform the French of this definite instruction.'

In fact, numbers of French and Belgium ships arrived during the 31st. The French destroyer *Léopard*, two French trawlers, three French motor fishing vessels and ten Belgium trawlers as well as French cargo ships had all reached Dunkirk. One of the French trawlers, *Pierre*, was carrying munitions and exploded when hit by a German shell.

Safely home. The original caption to this image, dated 31 May 1940, states that it shows some of the men landed that day at one of the Kent ports having arrived, 'still smiling', in London by train.

A welcome break as troops rest in a camp set up after their evacuation from Dunkirk.

It was the German artillery that caused Tennant the most problems throughout the 31st, with the German gunners maintaining a heavy and continuous bombardment of the beach and the inshore boats at La Panne. At 10.44 hours, Tennant signalled that, 'We have been continually, heavily bombarded and they [the Germans] are gradually finding the range of our loading berth.'[12]

Tennant decided that he could not risk ships waiting idly for long periods of time for men to be transported to them. He therefore limited the number of ships going inshore so that they could be quickly filled by the boats. Of these boats, sixteen were either sunk or disabled by shells or 'misadventure', such as grounding, swamping, machine failure or striking wreckage.

The shelling seriously affected the rate of embarkation at La Panne which slowed to a trickle of about 150 an hour. The German artillery was so effective because of two observation kite balloons which had been deployed above Nieuport. Tennant called for Fighter Command to shoot these down, but when the RAF appeared the balloons were hauled down only to be released back into the sky as soon as the fighters had flown away. One attempt at bringing down the balloons was made by six Hurricanes, only for them to be engaged by around thirty Bf 109s.

The hope was that as soon as night fell the German guns, denied their aerial observation, would be less accurate and the remaining 7,000 troops at La Panne would be lifted before the German guns recommenced their barrage at dawn. The dark, though, brought confusion, with large numbers of men crowding around the beach and scores of little boats skidding around the shallows. Wake-Walker was at La

Panne, 'wondering how things were going. Everything was black, ships and boats and shore showed no lights.' The messages he was receiving were contradictory, with ships masters claiming that their boats could find no men on the beach, whilst from the shore the news was that there were thousands of men on the beach and no boats to be seen. 'The ships and the boats were there,' declared a baffled Wake-Walker, 'and the troops ashore, and one could do no more … I do not know to this day,' he conceded, 'what really took place there.'[13] Embarkation at La Panne was terminated at 02.00 hours.

THE BALANCE SHEET

As night fell on the 31st the order was given for the remnants of II Corps to withdraw from the perimeter and make their way to Bray-Dunes. Some of the men joined the long, patient queues lining up in front of the improvised piers to wait for the small boats to pick them up. Most, though, continued for a further ten miles to the Mole.

Also moving onto the beach that night was the headquarters of the 1st Division's 3 Brigade. Earlier in the day the men of the 1st Division had learnt that they were to form the rear-guard – the last to leave. To prepare for their last stand on the beach, it was suggested that Brigadier T.N.F. Wilson should take his headquarters down to Bray-Dunes to prepare for the final evacuation in two days' time. The brigade's journey to Bray-Dunes was recorded in the Brigade War Diary for that night:

'The scenery provided a … picture of the abomination of desolation. Ruined and burnt out houses … salt water spreading everywhere, vehicles abandoned, many of them charred relics of twisted metal on the roadside and overturned in the ditches. Light tanks and guns poking up … Horses

dead or dying for want of water. Here and there civilian or French Army corpses in the open. An unforgettable spectacle.'[14]

The corps commander Gort chose (or was persuaded by Major General Montgomery) to command the rear-guard, and oversee the final evacuation, was Major General Harold Alexander who had commanded the 1st Division, but who was told to take over the rump of I Corps and the final defence of Dunkirk. That evening Lord Gort left Dunkirk on HMS *Hebe* and Harold Alexander assumed command of the remnants of the BEF.

The day ended with 22,942 men being lifted from the beaches and 45,072 from the harbour and the Mole, making 68,014. As we have seen, there are many stories of periods of time when there were no ships available, yet this was the most successful day

Taken by a Luftwaffe airman in the aftermath of Operation *Dynamo*, this picture provides an aerial view of the improvised pier constructed on the beach at Bray-Dunes. The road along the seafront is now known as Digue de Mer in Bray, whilst the bandstand in the centre of the promenade in this picture is now the location of a memorial.

of the evacuation, with the greatest number of troops being rescued and only one large ship, the minesweeper *Devonia*, being sunk, though the destroyers *Vivacious* and *Hebe* were damaged and *Wolsey*, *Impulsive*, *Scimitar*, *Icarus* and *Malcolm* being involved in accidents. ✠

NOTES:
1. Ellis, p.227.
2. Quoted in Jackson, p.137.
3. Lord, pp.198-9.
4. ibid, p.199.
5. A total of 166 survivors were rescued by the corvette HMS *Widgeon*, fifty by the trawler *Wolves*, twenty-one by the trawler *Stella Dorado* and fifteen by the Polish destroyer *Blyskawica*.
6. TNA ADM 199/788A.
7. Quoted in Sebag-Montefiore, pp.412-3.
8. TNA ADM 234/360.
9. *Dunkirk – First-hand Account of One of the Small Boats*, quoted on the BBC WW2 People's War website.
10. TNA ADM 234/360.
11. Lord, p.192.
12. TNA ADM 199/789.
13. TNA ADM 234/360.
14. TNA WO 167/350.

DAY 7: 1 JUNE

Aware that the BEF was getting away, the Luftwaffe undertook its largest raids of the campaign.

The cold light of dawn revealed not a horizon filled with waiting ships, but an almost empty sea, most of the vessels heading for England. Even the small boats had moved westwards away from the reach of the German artillery at Nieuport. The ships would return later and the first day of June would see tens of thousands of troops evacuated, but until then the men had to endure a day of terror and frustration, under enemy attack from the sky unable to retaliate. All they could do was dig in, keep their heads down and hope.

La Panne was as deserted as the sea opposite, but at Bray there was still some loading taking place and it was to there that the troops were trudging along the sand. Corporal George Leger was with the 8th Battalion, Durham Light Infantry, which, with the 6th and 9th battalions, formed the 151st Brigade, reached the coast on 1 June:

'When we got to Dunkirk on Saturday, there was just a feeling of dejection, and we were that tired and filthy dirty. We were picked up in lorries on the outskirts and taken the last few miles, to drive through the people who were guarding the perimeter, you couldn't just walk through.

'They were fighting a rear-guard action, keeping the perimeter open for us. When we got through, we got out of our lorries and started walking through Dunkirk. It was one horrific sight. Machines, lorries, guns, armaments, strewn both sides of the road … I walked halfway along the beach and there were rows and rows of troops, five or six deep, right up to the water's edge, and there was an officer standing at the head of each one.'[1]

The Thames barge *Shannon*, having left Southend at 12.00 hours on 31 May with three other boats towed by the tug *Sun III*, arrived at Ramsgate at 17.15 hours that evening. The little convoy left for France on the morning of the 1st, spotting a lifeboat en route. Arthur William Joscelyne was on board *Shannon*:

'We saw a ship's boat full of soldiers, and they were resting on their oars. In front of it there was a smaller dingy, with about a dozen dark-skinned fellows in, who hardly spoke any English at all. They were part of a Spanish labour corps, and they had attached themselves to this ship's boat full of soldiers and they were doing all the work, rowing like mad, while these soldiers were sitting back and letting them pull it.'[2]

Sun III and its gaggle of boats reached the waters around Dunkirk at 12.30 hours on 1

TOP RIGHT: **Pictured at a railway at an undisclosed south coast port, men of the BEF smile for the camera following their evacuation from Dunkirk.**

June and was directed to two further boats overloaded with troops. 'The soldiers were not used to boats, and they all rushed to get on board,' continued Arthur Joscelyne:

'We could have capsized at any moment. An officer stood up in the bows and got his revolver out. He said, "I'll shoot the first man who makes a move before I give you permission to board. You will do it in an orderly manner." He stood there with his revolver, while we got about fifty of them on board. They were in such a state that they just lay down anywhere.

A couple of them threw their rifles overboard and said, "We shan't want these anymore".'

The tug boat took these troops on board and with 148 passengers loaded, Master F.W. Russell decided to return to England. Though damaged, *Shannon* reached Ramsgate on 2 June.

The owner of thirty-seven-foot motor yacht, *Curlew*, with a crew of an engineer and two naval ratings, also reached Dunkirk on 1 June:

'We were at the beach from 4.40 until 6.25 and this was the most uncomfortable hour and three-quarters that I have ever spent, because until we had got our troops aboard it was a question of putting our engines astern and ahead, astern and ahead, so as to hold the boat just clear of the sand. Meanwhile, we were bombed at intervals, and so were the troops waiting on the beach.'[3]

THE LUFTWAFFE ARRIVES

It was at 04.15 hours that the Luftwaffe again appeared in the skies above Dunkirk. Forty Stukas attacked the shipping at sea. Fighter Command's 11 Group squadrons were soon in the air, flying a total of 267 sorties in eight missions throughout the day. But the RAF could not be present all the time, and the Luftwaffe had long periods in which it could operate freely against the beaches and the boats.

Abandoned vehicles and equipment litter the seafront at Dunkirk in the immediate aftermath of Operation *Dynamo*. The abandoned Thames sailing barge in the centre background is believed to be *Ethel Everard*, which had been towed across the Channel by the tug *Sun XII* in company with another barge, *Tollesbury*. The building in the distance with the round tower is the Malo Terminus Casino.
(All images Historic Military Press unless stated otherwise)

After disarming the depth charges and jettisoning them along with its torpedoes, *Keith* was abandoned. Vessels nearby rushed to help as more bombs were aimed at the destroyer, dropping amongst the men struggling in the water. Slowly the men were picked up by tugs, the minesweeper *Salamanca*, a skoot and the motor barge *Sherfield*. But an unidentified grey yacht was hit and sunk as it was collecting survivors – an anonymous victim, crewed by courageous volunteers, their names lost to posterity.

In a further raid at around 09.40 hours *Keith* was attacked by approximately fifty enemy aircraft and the destroyer sunk

In the first raid the main target was the destroyer HMS *Keith*, from which Wake-Walker was directing operations. The warship's manoeuvrability was severely restricted in the shallow waters but she managed to avoid being hit. However, what was believed to have been a delayed-action bomb exploded immediately astern of the destroyer which caused the ship's wheel to jam. Temporary steering was rigged up, but by the time the next attack came, at around 08.00 hours, her anti-aircraft guns were out of ammunition and all the skipper, Captain E.L. Berthon, could do was turn the ship in tight circles as fast as the destroyer was able.

Three Stukas headed directly for *Keith* and Wake-Walker watched as the enemy's bombs plunged straight towards the destroyer. Able Seaman Reginald Heron was on the warship's switchboard:

'There was a hell of a crash and everything shook like hell. We knew we'd been hit because we were more or less expecting it … A bomb from a Stuka went down the funnel, and blew out the whole of the underpart of the ship. We grabbed the codebooks, and put them in a specially-weighted bag and threw it over the side. Then someone shouted, "Abandon ship! Throw everything floatable overboard". So I threw a dan-buoy overboard … I jumped in behind it and started swimming with one arm. I swam over to a tug a few hundred yards away and grabbed hold of a rubber tyre on the side.'[4]

Able Seaman Heron was one of the lucky ones. A hole had been blown in the side of the destroyer below the waterline at the forward end of the starboard engine room. At the same time, the bulkhead between there and the boiler room was ruptured, allowing the sea to pour in, drowning those inside. A fire then started in the boiler room. *Keith* was hit two more times on the port side and she took on a severe list.

amidst a salvo of bombs. The last survivors, struggling to stay alive in the destroyer's oil slick, were not picked up until around 11.00 hours. Three officers and thirty-three men were lost.[5]

Another destroyer, HMS *Ivanhoe*, was also attacked as she was leaving the beaches with 1,000 soldiers on board. In the early hours of

TOP LEFT: **Skippered by Captain Charles Parker, the Steam Tug *Challenge* first reached Dunkirk on 31 May, working into 1 June on this trip. She is pictured here leaving Shoreham-by-Sea on Saturday, 4 May 2013, en route to Southampton after a major refit.** (Courtesy of the Dunkirk Little Ship Restoration Trust)

ABOVE RIGHT: **Seen from the deck of *Challenge*, this is the Gravesend-based Watkins tug *Tanga* pictured towing small boats towards the beaches at Dunkirk. The hospital ship in the background, *Paris*, was sunk by German aircraft whilst crossing the Channel on 2 June 1940.** (Courtesy of Mick Wenban)

BELOW: **A tug tows a 'Little Ship', both loaded with evacuated Allied soldiers, into a South Coast port during Operation *Dynamo*. The yacht is believed to be named *Nydia* and which still survives under her original name.**

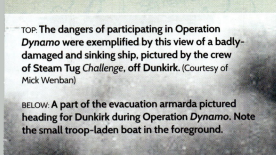

TOP: **The dangers of participating in Operation** *Dynamo* **were exemplified by this view of a badly-damaged and sinking ship, pictured by the crew of Steam Tug** *Challenge*, **off Dunkirk.** (Courtesy of Mick Wenban)

BELOW: **A part of the evacuation armarda pictured heading for Dunkirk during Operation** *Dynamo*. **Note the small troop-laden boat in the foreground.**

1 June she had gone to La Panne to find the beach deserted. She moved westwards where a large body of British troops had gathered. As the men were embarked, *Ivanhoe* was strafed repeatedly and subjected to high-level, but fortunately inaccurate, bombing.

After loading the troops *Ivanhoe* moved off, but as she was passing Dunkirk she was straggled by two bombs. A third hit the port whaler's after davit and exploded a few feet above the upper deck near the base of the foremost funnel.[6]

The No.2 Boiler room was pierced by bomb splinters, damaging the boiler and causing a fire which began to spread. Many of the deck fittings were destroyed and the ship's secondary armament was put out of action. She avoided further attention from the Luftwaffe by igniting a smoke-float in the bows which convinced the German pilots that the ship was severely crippled. Casualties were heavy, with twenty-six killed and thirty wounded. Most of the soldiers were taken off by HMS *Havant* which had berthed alongside the East Mole at 07.30 hours.

The Mole had become badly damaged by the incessant German shelling and aerial attacks. Gaps in the decking were covered with trestles, planks of wood, ladders and anything that could be found. The job of loading the troops was made even more difficult by the number of ships sunk alongside. There was, though, only a trickle of men in the early morning and after half an hour *Havant* had taken on board only about fifty men. Then, at around 08.00 hours, the Luftwaffe arrived overhead and *Ivanhoe* was seen to be hit and on fire.

Havant cast-off from the Mole and went to *Ivanhoe*'s assistance. She went alongside and took off approximately 500 men, some of whom were wounded. *Havant*'s captain, Lieutenant Commander A.F. Burnell-Nugent, then decided to make for Dover. 'On the way down the channel parallel to the beach to the west of Dunkirk we were subjected to intense dive bombing and high and low level bombing and also bombardment from shore,' reported Burnell-Nugent. 'These were avoided by zig-zagging as much as the width of the channel permitted. *Havant* had just turned to the North Westward at the end of the channel when, at 09.06, we were hit by two bombs in the Engine Room which passed through the starboard side. Almost immediately afterwards a large bomb fell in the water about 50 yards ahead. This had a delay ▶

One of a series of images taken by the crew of the Steam Tug *Challenge* **during Operation** *Dynamo* – **in this case a photograph of the view that greeted the tug's crew as they approached Dunkirk and its surroundings.** (Courtesy of Mick Wenban)

TOP: **Abandoned British Mk.VI Light Tanks on the beach between Malo-les-Bains and Dunkirk after the evacuation.**

BELOW RIGHT: **A pre-war picture of the minesweeper HMS *Saltash*, the presence of which was keenly felt off Dunkirk, especially in terms of assisting stricken ships, on 1 June 1940.** (Courtesy of the James Luto Collection)

action and exploded right underneath the ship as she passed over it, momentarily giving the impression of lifting the whole ship.'[7]

The destroyer was in serious trouble, approaching the sandbanks opposite Dunkirk. Somehow HMS *Havant* had to be stopped. This could only be done by letting steam out of the boilers, and Chief Stoker Gallor bravely stepped forward and let out the steam, even though there was a fire in one of the boiler rooms. *Havant* was eventually brought to a halt using the starboard anchor as a brake.

Signals for assistance were then made to HMS *Saltash* and a large private yacht. These came alongside one on each quarter and all the soldiers were transferred under almost continuous bombing. *Havant* was then taken in tow by *Saltash* but after another bomb had dropped between the two vessels it became clear that *Havant* was not going to make it back to England and it was decided to abandon ship. With her magazines flooded, *Havant* rolled over and sank at 10.15 hours, a few rounds having been fired into her by *Saltash*.

MORE LOSSES

It was not just the ships at sea off the beaches that came under attack. At 10.09 hours the SS *Prague*, which had earlier suffered damage from the German artillery, had loaded 3,000 French troops from the East Mole and set off for England when she was attacked by Ju 87s, suffering three very near misses which put the starboard engine out of action. The troops were transferred to other ships, most of these being taken on board the paddle minesweeper *Queen of Thanet*. *Prague* was taken in tow by the tug *Lady Brassey*, which attempted to get her back to Folkestone; but as she was in danger of sinking, she was beached at Deal. Over the course of four days *Prague* had rescued more than 6,000 soldiers from Dunkirk.

The losses continued to mount. The paddle minesweeper *Brighton Queen* arrived at Dunkirk at 10.35 hours having been under constant attack for the previous hour. She collected 700 French colonial troops and set off back to Margate thirty minutes later. Just as she started on Route X, *Brighton Queen* was attacked by a formation of Ju 87s and a 500-pound bomb exploded close to her starboard quarter, blowing a hole in her side. Water poured into the paddle steamer and she began to sink quickly. The minesweeper *Saltash* sped to *Brighton Queen*'s assistance and was able to save around 400 men, but the rest of the French troops were lost.

Another image taken from *Challenge* whilst en route to Dunkirk, this picture shows a passing coaster full of Allied troops rescued from Dunkirk. (Courtesy of Mick Wenban)

Close behind *Brighton Queen* was the SS *Scotia* which had also picked up French troops, in her case some 2,000 men. She too came under attack from the Stukas and at least four bombs hit her and she began to sink by the bows. The destroyer *Esk*, with guns blazing, came to *Scotia*'s rescue, driving off her attackers. *Esk* took on board approximately 1,000 men and HMS *Worcester* collected a few more, but twenty-eight of *Scotia*'s crew were lost, as were 200 or 300 of the French soldiers.

French ships also suffered when, at approximately 10.30 hours, the destroyer *Foudroyant* was hit by two consecutive salvos of bombs as it approached Dunkirk. She blew up and sank within two and a half minutes. Later in the day, at 16.00 hours, a convoy of French minesweeper trawlers, which was returning to Dunkirk after landing troops in England, was attacked by dive bombers. In the space of just five minutes, three of them, *Denis Papin*, *Venus* and *Moussaillon*, were lost.

On what the Admiralty called 'this black day', thirty-one vessels were sunk, including three Royal Navy destroyers, and eleven were damaged. Yet these bleak figures hide the true story of the day, which was that almost as many men had been landed in England as had been on 31 May. From the beaches 17,348 men had been saved, as well as 47,081 from the East Mole, giving a total of 64,429. These figures were further broken down by the Admiralty to show that motor boats and small craft had rescued 2,334 men, hopper barges had collected 1,470, private yachts 1,831, skoots 3,170, special service vessels 1,250, drifters 2,968 and trawlers had saved 1,876. French ships lifted 3,967, Belgian trawlers 402 and a Dutch yacht took 114.

One reason for such success was that the rate of embarkation was considerably increased during the day due to improved organisation. The destroyer *Vivacious*, for example, spent only fifteen minutes at the East Mole to collect 475 men, and *Shikari* needed only twenty minutes to take on board 623 troops.

Amongst those fortunate to reach England on 1 June was Lionel Tucker,

This small plaque on *Challenge's* bridge serves as reminder of her part in the Dunkirk evacuation.

who was serving with the RAOC as a motor engineer and attached to the 1st Battalion Oxford and Buckinghamshire Light Infantry:

'After spending a day trying to get aboard a boat of any kind without success an officer with a pistol in his hand ordered a large number of us to leave the beach and make our way to the 'Mole' which we found already packed with hundreds of troops.

'The trek to the end of the 'Mole' was disastrous, Jerry came over and made a direct hit causing many casualties, also a long delay in proceeding any further along.

'Eventually the gap was bridged and we were able to proceed, at that point I decided to remove all my webbing and equipment into the sea in case I had to swim for it. Eventually our saviour was in sight, a fairly large ship which I learnt later was the 'Maid of Orleans'. By this time I had lost any idea of time and was thoroughly exhausted, got on board, flopped down on deck amongst the others and fell fast asleep, I remember nothing about the journey until

I had a friendly kick from someone saying, "On your feet mate we are in Dover", I really couldn't believe what I was hearing was true. This was 0945hrs on the 1st of June 1940.'[8]

It was only because of the stubborn resistance of the soldiers holding the perimeter that so many men had been saved. Captain Harold Marcus Ervine-Andrews commanded a company of the 1st Battalion, East Lancashire Regiment which had been ordered to take over approximately 1,000 yards of the defences along the line of the Canal de Bergues. Ervine-Andrews later told of his experiences: 'I went up there on the evening of the 31st May to relieve one of my companies, D Company of my regiment. We knew we were in for a big attack the next day

A different collection of abandoned Mk.VI Light Tanks on the beach east of Dunkirk. Note the machine-gun in the foreground, and the tug in the background.

because all that day D Company had been having it pretty hard and at dawn on the 1st June the enemy attacked.'

The Dunkirk perimeter was hardly distinguishable as a defensive line, being nothing more than an irregular chain of strong points. This meant that the intense artillery barrage put down by the Germans for some two or three hours had comparatively little effect and the East Lancs were able to hold back the enemy throughout the morning. One of Ervine-Andrews' forward posts, however, was running desperately short of ammunition. This was ▶

A number of abandoned British Mk.VI Light Tanks, and a lone Universal Carrier, on the beach between Malo-les-Bains and Dunkirk pictured surrounded by German troops immediately after the end of *Dynamo*. The wreck in the background is, once again, that of the French destroyer *L'Adroit*.

A view of the French Navy's *Chasseur 9* stranded on the beach at Malo les Bains at the end of Operation *Dynamo*. Note the Universal Carrier in the foreground. In similar views, it is possible to see the Regina Hotel and the Guynemer statue in the right background.

BELOW RIGHT: A handwritten caption in German on the rear of this image states that it shows abandoned British military vehicles on a canal bank on the outskirts of Dunkirk during the evacuation in May and June 1940.

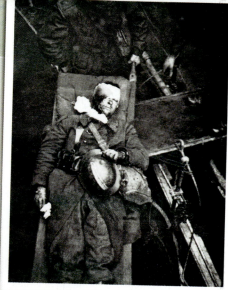

ABOVE: A wounded French soldier is disembarked at Dover having been successfully evacuated from Dunkirk.

because during the retreat to Dunkirk, the men had been instructed to dispose of surplus ammunition and the supply dumps on the lines of communications had been destroyed to prevent their contents falling into the hands of the enemy. The men of the East Lancs, in particular, had been ready to embark when they were 'whipped up' and ordered back to the perimeter, and they had to search amongst dead bodies around to try and find ammunition for their rifles.

Under mounting pressure, the East Lancs held on, but the shortage of ammunition became increasingly grave. The Germans had also succeeded in crossing the canal on both flanks and one of his sections was cut off, as Ervine-Andrews related: 'One of my sections was in a very, very, very, very, bad way. They had had a tremendous onslaught onto them, they were running very short of ammunition and they sent back and asked for urgent help and I looked round and I had no reserves whatsoever so I looked at the few soldiers who were with me in the company headquarters and said "look I am going up who's coming with me?", I said "give me that rifle" and I picked up a rifle and some ammunition and every single man there came forward with me. We went up, took over the position and the Germans had been lulled into a false sense of security and we were able then to hold up the attack on the position, and we held then for quite a long time until we ran out of ammunition.'

What Ervine-Andrews didn't say, was that the strong point he and his few men held was in a small barn across from the canal. The terrain, according to Ervine-Andrews, was 'pretty good it was low lying, low land, intersected by dykes with very, very, few farm buildings here and there and a few folds in the ground but a very open area which gave me personally a very good field of fire'. Ervine-Andrews used that good field of fire to great effect by mounting the roof of the barn from where he could pick off the enemy with his rifle. It is believed that he personally accounted for seventeen Germans with his rifle before taking over a Bren gun in the barn and killing many more.

Though a company commander, Ervine-Andrews took it upon himself to fire most of the depleted stock of ammunition. He explained his reason for doing this in a later interview: 'We had the dominant position in that they were out in the open. I was in a barn, they didn't know where I was and

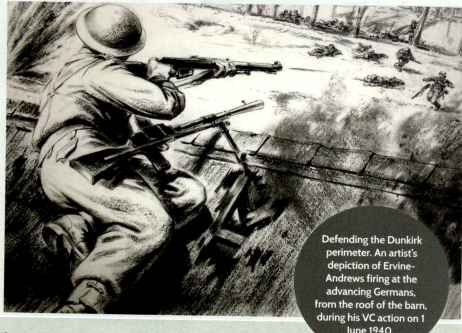

Defending the Dunkirk perimeter. An artist's depiction of Ervine-Andrews firing at the advancing Germans, from the roof of the barn, during his VC action on 1 June 1940.

it's all very, very, quick when you are firing ammunition and if you fire accurately and you hit men they are discouraged. It's when you fire a lot of ammunition and you don't do any damage the other chaps are very brave and push on. But when they are suffering severe casualties they are inclined to stop or as in this case they move round to the flanks because there is no point in going up and getting a bloody nose if you can avoid it by going round to a weaker position on either flank. Which is what the Germans did.'

The odds were too great for Ervine-Andrews' little band which eventually could do no more. With the burning barn having been all but blown to pieces and the men finally out of ammunition, they succumbed to the inevitable. Ervine-Andrews had held the position along the perimeter for more than ten hours – effectively holding up the Germans for a full day. He sent his wounded back in a

carrier and then, with his remaining eight men, he tried to lead his men back to the beach.

By this time his party was cut off from the rest of the BEF and all but surrounded. Taking advantage of any cover, they also had to swim or wade up to their chins in water along the canal for more than a mile to escape. Yet, thanks to Ervine-Andrews' determination, they made it through rough enemy lines to the blood-soaked beaches and finally escaped back to England three days later.

It is with little wonder that Harold Ervine-Andrews was recommended for the Victoria Cross. His citation in *The London Gazette* stated: 'Throughout this action, Captain Ervine-Andrews displayed courage, tenacity, and devotion to duty, worthy of the highest traditions of the British Army, and his magnificent example imbued his own troops with the dauntless fighting spirit which he himself displayed.'[9]

Ervine-Andrews' heroics may have been exceptional, but acts of courage were repeated along the perimeter as German pressure increased. The defenders were forced to give ground but, by nightfall, the line had been stabilized, the perimeter then running from Bergues to Ghyvelde and then along the Belgian frontier to the sea. The French had more than played their part, with General Janssen's 12th Division holding off a systematic attack by Kuechler's forces along the Belgium border. The months spent building defences throughout the previous winter proved not to have been wasted after all. The few tanks left with Kuechler had also been stopped by the French; General Beaufrère's artillery firing over open sights each time a panzer rumbled into view.[10] The RAF had also experienced success, shooting down six enemy aircraft.

Much would depend on Fighter Command and the French over the course of the next two days as the British rear-guard took up its final positions and the last men prepared to escape. There were still thousands of men in and around Dunkirk. If the Germans broke through the perimeter there would still be a bloodbath on the beaches. ✦

NOTES:
1. IWM, Department of Sound, Acc. 16722.
2. IWM, Department of Sound, Acc. 9768.
3. Quoted on the BBC Archive website: www.bbc.co.uk/archive/dunkirk
4. IWM, Department of Sound Acc. 22385.
5. TNA ADM 234/360.
6. TNA ADM 199/786.
7. ibid.
8. Lionel Tucker *Memories of The Maid of Orleans*, BBC WW2 People's War.
9. Supplement to *The London Gazette*, 26 July 1940. Lord, p.234.

TOP: **Abandoned vehicles and equipment litter a similar river crossing to that defended by Captain Ervine-Andrews and his men. The street sign in the background in this view looking north indicates that this is the spot where the D302 crossed the canal to the immediate south of Zuydcoote – two bridges east from the East Lancs' position. In this view, the Allied positions were located on the opposite side of the canal to the photographer, a German serviceman.**

BOTTOM: **A busy scene in the English Channel as ships of all shapes and sizes, military and civilian, make their way back to the South Coast laden with their valuable cargoes of evacuated Allied troops.**

After the heavy losses to shipping on 1 June, and the fact that the only route that had not been dominated by enemy artillery, Route X, was now coming under fire from German guns, it was decided to abandon daylight evacuations. But with part of I Corps, two French divisions and the 4,000 men of the rear-guard still to be lifted, a great effort was to be made during the night of 1-2 June.

It was hoped in London that the evacuation would continue until all the troops had been rescued, but because so many men had been drowned by enemy action on the 1st, it was accepted that a point would be reached where it was more dangerous for the troops to attempt evacuation than to try and save themselves or surrender.

The decision when to terminate Operation *Dynamo* was left to the men on the spot, this being communicated by General Ironside on the evening of the 1st: 'We do not order any fixed moment for evacuation. You are to hold on as long as possible in order that the maximum number of French and British may be evacuated. Impossible from here to judge local situation. In close co-operation with Admiral Abrial you must act in this matter on your own judgement.'[1]

By using both sides of the East Mole as well as the beaches, it was estimated that between 21.00 hours and 03.30 (this being the last time ships could depart Dunkirk and get safely past the German guns before daylight) 17,000 men could be evacuated. To enable this, the troops were to concentrate by the Mole and one and a half miles to the east. All minesweepers, as well as skoots and small craft were to operate off the beaches, as well as about 100 small French vessels such as beach fishing boats, whilst seven personnel ships and eight destroyers were to use the East Mole.

The French troops were mostly posted to the west of Dunkirk, and drifters and MTBs were to go into the inner harbour to lift these soldiers from the West Quay, whilst small private boats used the Quay Félix Faure. The destroyers were to operate in pairs and the Admiralty ordered that these ships should continue to operate from the Mole until 07.00 hours. Predictably, not all the vessels reaching Dunkirk were aware of these instructions and some embarkation continued during the day.

As mentioned before, the owner of a Thames launch, *Curlew*, set off for Dunkirk on 1 June, arriving in French waters during the night of 1-2 June. With him was his friend and two young Naval seamen lent as deckhands. He later wrote

BELOW: **A depiction of how the beaches at Dunkirk may have appeared in daylight – this, in fact, being a picture taken during the production of the 1958 film *Dunkirk*, directed by Leslie Norman and starring John Mills, Richard Attenborough and Bernard Lee.** (All images Historic Military Press unless stated otherwise)

DAY 8: 2 JUNE

It was hoped that this day would see the last troops lifted from the East Mole and the beaches – providing the perimeter held.

of his experiences: 'As we made our way up the channel leading to the port we could see the flashes from the artillery holding the coast and a vast pall of smoke hung over the town itself. One of our destroyers, apparently damaged, was tied up to the mole and firing furiously, but our orders were not to stop at the harbour but to push on past it to a beach about two miles to the east.

'The whole place was littered with wrecks, and the only vessels under way were *Cairngorm* and ourselves. *Cairngorm* sounded her way carefully towards the beach, and we were able to follow in her wake at full speed. So we drew up to her and both of us went alongside a pair of Thames barges, the *Glenway* and the *Lark*, which were aground and apparently deserted. But they made good landing-stages for us, though we could not tie up because of the danger of to grounding on the ebbing tide. Had we touched bottom we probably could not have got off again.

'We were at the beach from 4.40 until 6.25 and this was the most uncomfortable hour and three-quarters that I have ever spent, because until we had got our troops aboard it was a question of putting our engines astern and ahead, astern and ahead, so as to hold the boat just clear of the sand. Meanwhile, we were bombed at intervals, and so were the troops waiting on the beach.

'It had been our plan, had there been any destroyers or other large vessels nearby, to put our troops aboard them and go ashore for more, but the only other vessel was the destroyer that was firing shells from her berth at the mole … So we had no option but to make off for Ramsgate with our load of troops.'[2]

Another small craft that reached Dunkirk during the night was *Elvin*, a six-berth, thirty-six-foot 'gentleman's' motor yacht, which went to France under Lieutenant Commander Archie Buchanan: 'We lay off the entrance until first light. We could hear gunfire to the eastward and saw a great pall

of smoke over the town and flashes in the inner harbour. As soon as we could see we went alongside the eastern pier where a column of soldiers was drawn up. An officer called out '*Combien de soldats?*', and as I could not remember the French for twenty-five I replied '*Trente*', but before we could take on the thirty that had been detailed by the officer the sub rushed up from below and said that we were full.'[3]

After speaking to a Royal Navy sub-lieutenant in a small open motor boat, Buchanan decided to try and take the soldiers out to a destroyer, but when he sailed out of the harbour he found that all the destroyers had gone: 'So we chased after some French minesweepers to westward hoping to put our soldiers on board, but they were unable to take them so decided to set course for Ramsgate. We had no idea where the swept channel was, but as we drew only three feet six inches and it was not low water we didn't think that there was much danger from mines.' ▶

A view of one of the Thames barges left stranded on the beaches east of Dunkirk after the end of Operation *Dynamo* – note the German soldier sat in the cab of the vehicle in the foreground. The name on the bows indicates that this is *Aidie*. A sailing barge of 144 tons, *Aidie* was run ashore on 1 June by her skipper, C. Webb, and abandoned after food, water and ammunition had been unloaded – the same fate as her sister barge *Barbara Jean*. Some accounts state that *Aidie* was also set alight.

'We huddled together in the sand-dunes for protection from constant bombing and machine-gunning. To complete this nightmare scene, there was smoke coming from the oil tanks on fire at Dunkirk. At dawn the next day we were marshalled in groups of fifty by an officer or senior N.C.O., and marched down to the water's edge, where discipline was maintained by a naval beachmaster. Each group was called in turn – woe betide anyone who stepped out of line and tried to go out of turn! I saw one group run out of line and the person in charge was promptly shot by the beachmaster.

'Owing to the shallow draft of the beach, the first job was getting on to a rowing boat which took us a little way out, and where we were transferred to a launch which then took us to the larger vessels laying further off. On the way out to the bigger ships, our launch was bombed, and although we didn't suffer a direct hit, one bomb hit the water close enough to us to swamp the boat and I found myself in the water … I surfaced and looked around and saw there was a ship closer to me than the shore, so I struck out for her. She was a converted minesweeper called the *Medway Queen*. I was hauled out of the water totally exhausted – so were my mates.'[4]

Medway Queen left Dunkirk at 02.45 hours with 426 soldiers on board, and on the way back to England picked up ten Spanish labour force men, and the crews of two motor boats whose engines had broken down.

Elvin survived the return trip and has also survived the ravages of time and still sails today as a proud member of the Association of Dunkirk Little Ships.

The Hunt-class minesweeper HMS *Lydd* reached Dunkirk just before midnight on 1 June. Her skipper was Lieutenant Commander Rodolph Cecil Drummond Haig: 'The beach and roads were being shelled, and there did not appear to be much boat traffic. I sent the motor boat inshore and it brought off the Brigadier of the Brigade then embarking, who asked that a message from the acting C-in-C might be sent to V.A. Dover [Ramsay] asking that the embarkation should be diverted to the beach, as French soldiers were causing congestion on the piers. It was also stated that the rearguard would arrive about 0230. I informed V.A. Dover and all the forces at Dunkirk of this by W/T. The difficulty at the beach appeared to be lack of boats. With *Lydd*'s boats about two hundred were embarked by 0245, 2nd June.'

Amongst those that get back to the UK on 2 June was Albert Powell, a driver with the Royal Signals attached to III Corps Medium Artillery Headquarters. His unit had been heavily bombed on 24 May at Poperinghe, the commanding officer being killed. During the retreat to Dunkirk the unit had become dispersed and by the time Albert reached the beaches on 1 June there was only three other men with him:

LEFT: **Abandoned ships, vehicles and other debris on the beach at Dunkirk, possibly in the area of Malo-les-Bains. The vessel on the left appears to be the schoot *Horst*. Commanded by Lieutenant Commander G. Fardell RN, having previously been lying at Poole, *Horst* had transported 1,150 men before running aground near the West Mole on 3 June and abandoned.**

This picture provides a clear indication of the scale of the destruction wrought on Dunkirk during May and June 1940. This is the Rue du Kursaal.

LEFT: **The Tug *Fossa*, with a Thames sailing barge beyond, lies stranded east of Dunkirk. According to the historian Russell Plummer, *Fossa* towed a number of vessels across the Channel, including the ketch *Jeanette* with which *Fossa* then worked loading troops from the East Mole. When *Jeanette* developed a steering fault, *Fossa* herself went in, towing *Jeanette* and a naval cutter. *Fossa* then ran aground and cast off the tows, the men on board being transferred to another boat. *Fossa* was refloated but reported lost on 2 June after suffering a direct hit.**

BELOW: **A Junkers Ju 52 overflies the beach to the east of Dunkirk after the end of Operation *Dynamo*. The beached vessel in the foreground is, once again, the tug *Fossa*.**

The first large ship to sail from Malo-les-Bains on 2 June was the paddle-steamer *Emperor of India*, which set off back to the UK at 02.38 hours with 213 troops.

As the destroyers (and a few other vessels unaware of the order to restrict evacuations to night time) would be passing the German batteries in daylight, the RAF was asked to help, and twenty-four sorties by Blenheims were directed to the area near Pointe de Gravelines. They operated from first light until 07.45 hours, when the last of the destroyers should have passed the crucial spot.

After the heavy attacks by the Luftwaffe the previous day, Fighter Command put five full squadrons into the air over Dunkirk on the 2nd. The Spitfires and Hurricanes claimed eighteen enemy bombers and ten fighters, for the loss of just seven of their own machines. Further air protection was provided by Coastal Command and the Fleet Air Arm between 08.30 hours and 11.00 hours by aircraft from Nos. 206, 235, 801 and 806 squadrons.

The Allies also took to the offensive on the ground, with the bridgehead the Germans had established on the north bank of the Bergues-Furnes canal being driven back over the water by the 21e Centre d'instruction divisionnaire supported by six Somua 35 tanks.

After the evacuations of the morning just how many troops remained in and around Dunkirk was not known with any degree of precision. It was thought that there might only be 2,000, plus the 4,000 rear-guard British troops, though the number of French troops remaining was increasing by the hour and was now in the region of 50,000 to 60,000.

At 10.30 hours an urgent request was sent to Ramsay from Dunkirk for Hospital Carriers: 'Wounded situation acute and Hospital Ships should enter during day. Geneva Convention will be honourably observed it is felt and that the enemy will refrain from attacking.'[5] As this appeared to be the only way of evacuating the wounded, observing that the whole facilities of the port during the night evacuation hours would be required for fighting troops, it was decided to send two Hospital Ships, hoping that, indeed, the Germans would not attack them.

The first to head for Dunkirk was *Worthing*, which sailed at 13.00 hours, followed by *Paris* four hours later. At 14.40 hours *Worthing*, which was about two-thirds of the way across the Channel, was attacked by twelve Ju 87s. There were no casualties but she suffered some superficial damage and returned to England.

Then, at 19.15 hours, *Paris* reported that she had also been attacked at roughly the same point as *Worthing*. She had been ▶

A German propaganda postcard depicting the scene on a stretch of the beach at Dunkirk after the evacuation. In the foreground appears to be a Renault UE Chenillette light tracked armoured carrier, whilst in the background there are three improvised piers.

LEFT: Oberleutnant Heinrich Braumann was one of the many Germans who eventually broke into Dunkirk once the evacuation ended. He kept a photographic record of his participation in the Blitzkrieg. This photograph was one he took on the outskirts of Dunkirk, his original caption stating: 'Countless destroyed English vehicles clog the village streets.' Note the dunes in the background, suggesting that this picture was taken just behind the beaches to the east of the port.

BELOW: 'For the last 20km of our advance on Dunkirk the streets had been littered with English war materiel', wrote Oberleutnant Braumann beneath this picture. The presence of the overhead electricity wires and gantries for a tram or railway, and the high sandy dunes beyond, suggest that this photograph might have been taken in the vicinity of Bray-Dunes to the east of Dunkirk itself. Located on the border with Belgium, Bray-Dunes is the northern-most point in all of France.

bombed and badly damaged with her engines rendered useless. At 19.47 hours, she sent out an S.O.S., and tugs were sent to her assistance. This meant that the last attempt to evacuate the wounded by Hospital Carrier from Dunkirk had failed. *Paris* subsequently sank shortly after midnight on 3 June, ten miles off the French coast. Ramsay informed the Admiralty of these attacks by the Luftwaffe, making it plain that the circumstances admitted 'of no mistake of their identity'.

This placed the men of the Royal Army Medical Corps to the mercy of the enemy, knowing that if they wanted to escape to England they would have to leave their wounded and, in all too many cases the dying. This, these courageous doctors, nurses, assistants, orderlies and drivers simply could not do. Many would stay with their patients. They knew that in doing so they would inevitably be taken prisoner.

The 11th Casualty Clearing Station had set up its operating rooms at La Panne, which was soon to be overrun. Rather than let all the staff be captured, the colonel in charge decided that it was only necessary for one doctor and ten orderlies to remain for every 100 patients. The question of who remained was settled by drawing lots.

THE LAST ESCAPE

Motor Anti-Submarine boat, *MASB 6*, commanded by an unnamed officer was sent to look for the drifter *Girl Gladys*, which had been reported broken down seven miles east of Dunkirk. After picking up eighteen soldiers from an open boat, *MASB 6* continued along the French coast looking for *Girl Gladys*:

'At approximately 1720 when out of sight of land we were attacked by either six or eight dive-bombers, 20 to 30 bombs were dropped and fell at distances varying from 10 to 50 yards of the ship. The bombers appeared to attack in pairs out of the sun and having released their bombs continued their dive firing machine-guns.

'Course was altered frequently in an endeavour to miss the bombs. Some appeared to explode after entering the water, some on striking the surface and a certain number appeared not to explode at all. One exploded under the bow right ahead and the ship passed through the splash. A certain amount of discomfort was experienced by myself and members of the crew who were exposed to the splash in the eyes for the next twelve hours or so.

BELOW: German personnel use horses to recover abandoned military vehicles from the beaches east of Dunkirk in the aftermath of Operation *Dynamo*. A handwritten note on the rear states that picture was taken by a German soldier in July 1940. The vehicle appears to be a Renault UE Chenillette light tracked armoured carrier – possibly being that depicted in the drawing on the bottom of page 85. The wreck in the distance is that of the steamship *Lorina*. On 29 May *Lorina* was off the beaches when she was caught in a dive-bombing attack and suffered a direct hit amidships which broke her back, the vessel going down in shallow water despite the determined efforts of her skipper Captain A. Light to beach her. Eight crewmen lost their lives in the attack. With her flags still defiantly flying, the Southern Railway steamer became a point of navigation for other vessels taking part in the evacuation..

The scene at Dunkirk – a drawing by the artist F. Matania that appeared on the front of *The Sphere* on 8 June 1940.

Division, had attacked along the road to Spycker, while over to the east the 56th Infantry Division had tried to break through the positions held by the French 12th Division. In both instances the defenders had shown the kind of determination which saw them hold back the Germans for four years in the First World War. In the fighting, the 12th Division lost its fine commander, General Louis Janssen. Though the perimeter held in most sectors, a major assault upon Bergues, preceded by a heavy bombardment by Ju 87s, saw the town taken by Küchler's 18th Infantry Division. The Germans, however, were halted on the banks of the Canal des Moëres.

Meanwhile, Wake-Walker and the senior officers held back all the ships and boats that had approached Dunkirk until nightfall when they would be released for the mass descent upon the harbour and the beach. In preparation for the evening rush, minesweepers, destroyers, anti-submarine trawlers and drifters worked to ensure that the swept channel remained clear of any danger – yet this placed some of those vessels within range of the enemy. At 16.15 hours the anti-submarine trawler *Blackburn Rovers* was struck by a torpedo, probably fired from a small coastal submarine. Two other anti-submarine trawlers were also hit; *Spurs*, was bombed and severely damaged, and *Westella* was sunk by a torpedo – possibly from the same submarine that attacked *Blackburn Rovers*. These losses notwithstanding, the channel was rendered safe as evening approached.

'Able-Seaman Power was wounded in the leg when manning the port turret also one of the soldiers in the fore peak. As I now had wounded on board I considered it advisable to return to Dover forthwith … The bombing to which the ship had been subjected had caused leaks to the hull and the petrol tank and the ship was not used again for that night's operation.'[6]

At 15.38 hours, Tennant submitted a situation report to Ramsay in which he stated that in general the French were holding the perimeter and he declared 'Present situation hopeful'. If the French could hold the line until nightfall when the evacuation would recommence in earnest, the last of the BEF could well get away without too much resistance from the enemy.

In fact, the Germans had resumed their assault upon the perimeter just half-an-hour or so earlier when 61st Infantry Division, supported by tanks from the 9th Panzer

ABOVE: **The Porte de Bierne formed part of the defences of the Citadel of Bergues. It was a vital part of the Allied defence of the town during *Dynamo* – as evidenced by the damage that can still be seen (note the large repair on the left-hand tower).**

At 17.00 hours the movement of the great armada towards Dunkirk began. This collection of vessels consisted of thirteen personnel ships, two large store carriers, eleven destroyers, five paddle minesweepers, nine fleet minesweepers, one special service vessel, nine drifters, six skoots, two armed yachts and one gunboat. There was also a large number of tugs, lifeboats, and other 'Little Ships' formed either in organised tows or operating independently. The composition of the French contingent is unknown, it was thought to consist of six small destroyers, four despatch boats and about 120 fishing craft. ▷

ABOVE: **Evidence of the bitter fighting in 1940 can be seen on the walls of the Church of Saint-Éloi in Rue Clemenceau, Dunkirk.**

One of those who went in that evening was Sub-Lieutenant G.A. Cadell who had taken over command of HM Motor Boat *Lady Cable* earlier on 2 June from a Mr Goodall, who had operated the boat for the owner. Under Mr Goodall the boat had already undertaken one trip to Dunkirk. After taking on water, provisions and fuel, she was taken in tow by the tug *Sun VI*, together with two life-boats and one other craft, setting off for Dunkirk at approximately 15.30 hours. Sub-Lieutenant Goodall recalled what followed:

'After uneventful trip arrived off Dunkirk harbour at about 2230 and received orders to proceed in harbour and go a long way up the Mole to embark soldiers – fill up and return to tug, then go in for further loads. At times had difficulty in persuading French troops to embark in *Lady Cable*, the reason apparently being reluctance to break their units or to act without definite orders from their officer who was probably still in the town of Dunkirk. However, we took four boat loads off – each load containing between 40 and 50 soldiers. Three loads I took to tugs – and one to H.M.S. *Wishart* when tug was not in usual position.

A surviving 'Little Ship', the twin-screw schooner *Chico*. On 30 May, *Chico*, commanded by Sub-Lieutenant J. Mason, RNVR, left for Dunkirk where she embarked 217 troops before returning to Dover. On the 31st she ferried nearly 1,000 troops from the Dunkirk shore to ships, disembarking a further estimated 100 troops herself on her return to Dover. On 2 June, she was transferred to life-saving duties on Route X. (Courtesy of The Carlisle Kid, www.geograph.org.uk)

'Spoke to tug after forth trip and was informed that it would soon be light and that she couldn't wait much longer. In reply to a question if any British Officers were still left on the Mole, I replied that on earlier trips I had seen one who had asked me not to leave him behind. This Officer was engaged in helping the embarkation of the troops. I had not seen him on my last trip but told tug I would make another trip to see if he was there. Informed tug would be as quick as possible and if tug could not wait, would return to England under own power. Tug said she could only wait a short while.

'On going in for fifth time engines began to go badly and stopped altogether before

reaching point of embarkation. Engines got going again and we went alongside and collected about 24 more French soldiers. There was no sign of British Officer and Price reported to me that French on the Mole told him he had gone. I sent Price up on to the Mole to make enquiries. Owing to the improbability of tug waiting for us, I only took 24 soldiers as a greater number would have made trip back to England under own power too hazardous.'[7]

The evening evacuation went very smoothly with the shipping being well-controlled. There was, though, one unfortunate incident, involving the French cross-Channel ferry, *Rouen*. As the tide began to ebb, *Rouen*, which had collected a number of men from the harbour, became stranded on the mud. The tug *Foremost* went to help pull the French vessel clear but herself grounded and only just managed to reverse engines and get back into deeper water. A smaller tug, *Sun X*, then went in, but found that even 200 yards from *Rouen* there was only ten feet of water beneath her keel, and it was evident that *Rouen* could not be moved until the next tide.

The Porte de Cassel at Bergues after the end of Operation *Dynamo*. During the retreat to, and evacuation from, Dunkirk, British troops blocked the Porte de Cassel with an Army bulldozer. Here that bulldozer is pictured being removed by German personnel. Note the damage caused by the fighting in this location – much of which can still be seen today.

The Church of Saint-Éloi is next to the Place Jean Bart – a view of which, including abandoned Allied military vehicles and equipment, can be seen here. Note the statue to Jean Bart, which can still be seen in the square to this day, in the centre of the picture. The Church of Saint-Éloi is a short distance to the left of where the photographer was standing. A similar can be seen on page 36.

LEFT: **One of the many evacuated Allied soldiers, in this case a French infantryman (albeit wearing a British helmet), rests his weary feet during the journey across the Channel.**

ABOVE: **A wounded soldier on a stretcher is given a drink on the quayside at Dover, 31 May 1940.**

LEFT: **Members of a Merchant Navy crew or civilians, one of whom is wounded, are taken aboard a British ship during the evacuation from Dunkirk.**

Rear Admiral Taylor, who it may be recalled was the Maintenance Officer for *Dynamo* at Sheerness, whose work was done, decided to sail to Dunkirk to see if he could help with the evacuation from Malo-les-Bains, where the little boats he had prepared were due to operate. He crossed the Channel in the motor cruiser *White Wing*, on board which was David Devine:

'Having an Admiral on board, we were not actually working the beaches but were in control of small boat operations. We moved about as necessary and, after we had spent some time putting boats in touch with their towing ships, the 5.9 battery off Nieuport way began to drop shells on us. It seemed pure spite. The nearest salvo was about twenty yards astern, which was close enough. We stayed there until everybody else had been sent back and then went pottering about looking for stragglers.'[8]

At 21.45 hours it was learned that the former LNER train ferry *Royal Daffodil*, which had been converted to a landing ship, had been bombed near the North Goodwin Light Vessel on the outward passage from where she returned to England. When *Royal Daffodil* reached Ramsgate, a 16-year-old apprentice with the General Steam Navigation Company based at Deptford,

Tom Mogg, was asked to count all the bullet holes in the ship.

'There were thousands of them,' he recalled. 'When I walked into the ship, it was a bright sunny day outside, and it gave the impression that I was walking into a colander – there were so many shafts of light beaming in through the holes. We circled every bullet hole we found, measured it, and made a note of it. If the hole was more than two inches across it had to be fixed by a shipwright, less than two inches and it could be done by a carpenter.

'The *Royal Daffodil* had also been dive-bombed on its final crossing and the bomb had passed through three decks into the engine room, missing the fuel tank by inches, and exited the hull before it exploded. It had been a very lucky escape for those onboard. The captain had to instruct all the soldiers to move to the port side to try to raise the hole in the starboard side out of the water.'[9]

The Halcyon-class minesweeper HMS *Leda* set off from Dover at 16.45 hours and was off the entrance to Dunkirk Harbour by 23.00 hours. She went in and berthed against

LEFT: **A train full of evacuated soldiers, British and French, are welcomed at a stop during their journey inland away from one of the South Coast ports.**

the East Mole as German artillery shelled the harbour entrance. Not a single soldier was seen along the Mole, and, after fifty minutes, Lieutenant Commander Harold Unwin was ordered to slip his berth and return to the UK. He returned empty.

With the French stoutly holding the perimeter and darkness concealing movement, the rear-guard slipped away from their positions in front of the enemy and made its way towards Malo-les-Bains and the harbour.

By 23.00 hours most of the British troops had been embarked. The last unit to be lifted from Dunkirk was the 1st Battalion King's Shropshire Light Infantry, which departed on the Channel ferry *St Helier*, which slipped the East Mole at 23.00 hours. It was that moment when Captain Tennant despatched a short message to Dover. Though it was the briefest signal sent since *Dynamo* began, it was the most welcome message of all. It simply read: 'B.E.F. evacuated. Returning now.'[10]

NOTES:
1. Tennant's report in TNA ADM 199/789.
2. 'The *Curlew* at Dunkirk', quoted on the BBC Archive website:www.bbc.co.uk/archive/Dunkirk
3. Quoted in Robert Jackson, p.171.
4. Quoted in Knowles, pp.186-7.
5. Grehan and Mace, p.143.
6. TNA ADM 199/787.
7. ibid.
8. Divine, p.208.
9. 'I helped keep Dunkirk rescue ship afloat', *Bath Chronicle*, 26 May 2010.
10. This is the wording of Tennant's signal as recorded in the Admiralty's Battle Summary No.41, in TNA ADM 234/360. However, Dildy, p.80, writes that this has been reworded for posterity, the original signal reading being: 'Operation complete. Returning to Dover'.

DAY 9: 3 JUNE

The BEF had been saved to fight another day. But there were still large numbers of French troops at Dunkirk, so the ships and boats were asked to make one final effort.

On 2 June, a total of 26,265 men had reached the UK, of whom 6,695 had been lifted from the beaches and 19,561 from the harbour and the East Mole. A similar number would be rescued on the 3rd, mostly from the evacuation through the night of 2/3 June.

Amongst those vessels that joined in the evacuation that night was the Kingfisher-class Patrol Sloop HMS *Guillemot*, commanded by Lieutenant Commander Henry Maxwell Darrell-Brown. The

ship was off Dunkirk at 23.00 hours, and reached the Western Mole at 23.55:

'It was high water and owing to the shape of the Mole the ship could not lie close enough for the brow to reach. This difficulty was solved by heaving the bow in and utilising the flare of the bow. The ship secured past H.M.S. *Speedwell* which was lying at the outboard end of the Mole.

'There were about six hundred French troops ashore, and after thirty-one minutes of embarkation the ship was full, and cast off from

the Mole, leaving about two hundred troops behind. Boats were seen approaching the Mole and it was thought that the remaining troops would be collected by them. *Guillemot* cast off at 02.25. There was considerable congestion at the entrance and collision was with difficulty avoided. Aircraft flares were seen on the return journey but no attacks were made on the ship. Thick fog came down at daylight, and the ship anchored near the Foreland Buoy at 04.28 for one hour, arriving at Margate at 07.00 and disembarked 387 Officers and men.'

Fires were still burning when this German despatch rider made his way through the dock area at Dunkirk.

The skipper of the paddle steamer *Marmion* was Temporary Lieutenant H.C. Gaffney, who wrote a staccato report of his ship's actions on 3 June:

'Vessel under gunfire – aircraft active. Entered harbour 0100. Vessel alongside mole – considerable swell – no troops for some time – much shelling. Embarked 204 troops and told to clear off as no more troops arriving. Port paddle fouled by floating rope. Cleared harbour at 0233 – proceeded to Dover.'

The last of the vessels left Dunkirk at daybreak, leaving tens of thousands of French troops, as well as numerous British wounded, whose only hope of salvation was in being rescued by the Royal Navy and the Little Ships. But many of the crews had been working almost without respite since 26/27 May, and this was not just ordinary labour. They had to operate under bombardment from the sky and the land, with the decks of their ships crowded with soldiers, allowing little or no space for the crews, either volunteer civilian or naval, to rest or relax. It was even remarked upon by one Royal Navy officer that as the days wore on it was the crews who were looking more dishevelled and exhausted than the soldiers they were embarking.[1]

The crews had been pushed to the very limit but with what had been estimated to be as many as 30,000 men still to be saved, Ramsay knew every effort had to be made to try and rescue as many of them as he could in the hours that were left, not least because the actions of General Fagalde, and the men who had come under his command, had enabled the BEF to be saved. Ramsay was determined therefore that as many French troops as possible would be evacuated on the night of the 3rd, but he told the Admiralty that would be the end of *Dynamo*. He would not ask any more from the crews beyond that date. This was relayed to the French Admiralty, which agreed that one final effort would be made on the night of 3/4 June.

Even though there was still another night of evacuations to come, the original timetable for the blocking of Dunkirk's Inner Harbour, to render the port unusable by the enemy, was to be maintained. Admiral Abrial had asked if the blockade ships could arrive at Dunkirk at 03.00 hours on 3 June but when he was made aware of just how many French soldiers remained to be evacuated, he asked that the blockade be postponed. Ramsay, nevertheless, believed that the evacuation ▶

Taken by a German soldier in the immediate aftermath of Operation *Dynamo*, this picture shows abandoned British and French vehicles on the quayside in the harbour at Dunkirk, with, in the background, the East Mole or jetty that proved so important during the evacuation. (All images Historic Military Press unless stated otherwise)

charges exploded on *Westcove* she shifted off the mud and came to rest on her keel in mid channel. The result of the blockade attempt was that there was still a gap of some fifty feet through which ships could pass at highwater. This was one of *Dynamo*'s few failures.

THE FINAL NIGHT

With no daylight movement of shipping close to the French coast, it meant that the RAF could concentrate its efforts in a far narrower time-frame. Protection was therefore arranged by Coastal Command between Dover and Dunkirk from 19.30 hours until nightfall on the 3rd, and then on 4 June four squadrons from Fighter Command were to patrol from 04.30 hours until 06.15 hours, by which time it was expected that the last ships would be in home waters.

would be unaffected by blocking the Inner Harbour and so the blockade ships were ordered to sail as previously planned.

The three blockships, *Westcove*, *Edward Nissen* and the MV *Holland*, arrived at Dunkirk in the company of the destroyer HMS *Vivacious* and two MTBs. At 02.45 hours the blockships entered the harbour, just as a long line of destroyers was making its way out to sea. Concealed behind the destroyers was a large and fast transport ship which, appearing out of the semi-darkness, bore down on *Holland*. Even before she was hit, the skipper of *Holland*, knowing exactly what was going to happen, called out 'Abandon Ship!'. The transport crashed into *Holland* just before the boiler room bulkhead.

The ship went down by the bows almost immediately. Luckily, she was only in eight feet of water and all the crew were saved, though two were severely injured in the collision.

The other two blockships continued into the Inner Harbour. At the allotted point *Westcove* swung hard to starboard with the intention of smashing into the Inner West Jetty, but her bows got stuck in the mud while still fifty feet from the jetty. Likewise, *Edward Nissen* put her wheel about to charge into the East Jetty. Though the operation had not gone to plan, both crews fired their scuttling charges, but when the

TOP LEFT: *Oberleutnant* Braumann, who we have encountered before, took this picture of a member of his unit in turn photographing the debris on the beach at Dunkirk. His original caption stated: 'Overlooking the destroyed fleet at Dunkirk; in the background is the burning harbour.'

ABOVE RIGHT: Men of the British Expeditionary Force arriving at a British port, almost certainly Dover, after their evacuation from Dunkirk. One soldier assists a wounded comrade who walks with the aid of a stick. The soldier second from the left has been identified as Alec J. Harrison, a member of the Royal Army Medical Corps who 'was among the last soldiers to be evacuated'.

FAR LEFT: German soldiers pose for the camera on a British Army lorry abandoned on the seafront at Dunkirk.

NEAR LEFT: British sailors, wearing a strange assortment of civilian clothing, lined up on the platform of a London railway station after helping evacuate the BEF.

BELOW: Some of those left behind. *Oberleutnant* Braumann took this shot of 'a large group of French prisoners of war at Dunkirk'.

BOTTOM: The scene on the beach at Malo-les-Bains near the Malo Terminus Casino (visible on the far left), in the immediate aftermath of Operation *Dynamo*. From right to left, the ship wrecks are the tug *Fossa*, the steamship *Lorina*, and two Thames barges, *Aidie* and *Ethel Everard*. Note the remains of an improvised pier.

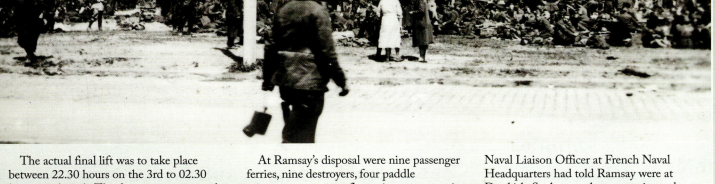

The actual final lift was to take place between 22.30 hours on the 3rd to 02.30 hours on the 4th. The destroyers, personnel ships, corvettes, skoots and paddle-steamers would operate from the East Mole. The ships were to use the full length of the Mole, being sent in and despatched as quickly as possible. There would be no time to hang around. The drifters and small craft were to go directly into Dunkirk Harbour, and any other British craft were to use the West Mole (called the New Avant Port). French vessels, of an unknown number, were to pick up any soldiers they found on the beach at Malo-les-Bains, the Quai Félix Faure and the West Mole.

At Ramsay's disposal were nine passenger ferries, nine destroyers, four paddle minesweepers, seven fleet minesweepers, nine drifters, and two corvettes. The Dragonfly-class river gunboat HMS *Locust* would also accompany the flotilla and would wait off Dunkirk where it would receive men ferried out to her from smaller vessels.

The French were to send craft to Dover during the day where they would be organized into flotillas for the crossing to Dunkirk for the night-time evacuation. In addition to this, four French torpedo boats were available.

This was enough shipping to embark the 30,000 French troops that the British

Naval Liaison Officer at French Naval Headquarters had told Ramsay were at Dunkirk. Such a number was estimated to be around 5,000 more than could be taken from Dunkirk harbour, the rest would have to be lifted from Malo beach. In reality, there was around double that number of French soldiers in and around Dunkirk. Many would be left behind.

The ships and boats gathered beyond Dunkirk as night fell. Then, at 22.00 hours, they were released and the rush began. 'The congestion [in the harbour] was chaotic,' wrote Lieutenant J.N. Wise in the skoot *Pascholl*. 'Ships going astern into others coming ahead. French destroyers ▶

TOP: **German personnel sitting at the top of the beach amongst abandoned British vehicles.**

shrieking on their sirens, small craft nipping here and there, rendering the exit most dangerous.'[2]

Wake-Walker had returned to Dunkirk to help with the final evacuation in MTB 102, and he also found the harbour 'swarming with French fishing craft and vessels of all sorts. They were yelling and crowding alongside the East Pier which was already thick with French troops. At one time it looked as if they would get in the way of the transports and destroyers which were on their way, but I managed to get them to go on up the inner harbour and out of the way in time.'[3]

H.M. Transport *Princess Maud* reached Dunkirk just before midnight. Forming part of the volunteer crew was Bill Birtles: 'Dunkirk was being shelled and bombed. The smoke was that thick, oily smoke blowing inland. We managed to dock at the mole with difficulty and by 2 am on the 4th

June we were overloaded with 2,200 British and French Army and Naval personnel. How we got out, God only knows. Harry [surname unrecorded] played a great part in marshalling them.

'One of the destroyers pulled us off by the stern and at 2.30 am we were clear, leaving stern first, out into the Channel and headed for Folkestone. We had to wait for high tide to get in. The troops were very restless, so near, yet so far. Harry took the loudhailer from the bridge and used it as only service men understood. He told them that they must be patient. We would be going on the tide within the hour.'[4]

The experiences of Lieutenant Commander George Anthony Mayhew Vaughan Harrison, of the Patrol Sloop *Kingfisher*, were in marked contrast to those of most of the British skippers: 'Went alongside West Pier, Dunkirk Harbour and embarked 210 French troops, who were

very well organised for embarkation, and appeared much fresher than any of our own. They also still possessed practically all their equipment.'

With so many vessels rushing in and out of the harbour it was probably inevitable that there would be accidents and *Kingfisher* was rammed by the French trawler *Edmond René*. The trawler ripped a hole in *Kingfisher*'s bows almost down to her waterline. In the collision, the two boats swung alongside each other and, as the trawler was undamaged, the French troops were transferred from *Kingfisher*. The sloop was able to limp slowly back to England.

Some indication of just how dangerous it was in the harbour can be gleaned from the report of Sub-Lieutenant Marwood J.B. Yeatman, who took over command of the Lowestoft lifeboat *Michael Stephens* on 2 June and was towed over to France by the tug *Sun XI*:

BELOW: **A German soldier pictured amongst the debris of war that littered the beaches east of Dunkirk. The planks in the foreground almost certainly formed part of a walkway on one of the improvised piers.**

ABOVE: **During August 1940, the King visited Southern Command and conferred the DSC and MC on a number of officers who distinguished themselves in the retreat to Dunkirk and subsequent evacuation. He is seen here inspecting a recently-returned unit of the Royal Field Artillery.**

'Entered harbour and went towards Eastern Mole. Rammed by M.T.B. without much damage. Went alongside Eastern Mole. With difficulty got 12 French soldiers aboard. Proceeded out to find tug which had disappeared, landed troops on trawler. Returned to harbour, being rammed by another M.T.B. on the way. Found Sloop (identification letters S.G. or S.C.). Owing to swish of tide she could not come alongside, so with the big engines of the lifeboat I pushed her alongside and went aboard to help make fast.

'Climbed on to Mole, which was being shelled, and by means of some forceful language and a rifle butt, induced the French troops who were lying on the Mole to start down on to the Sloop. Once a few had started they all began to go down. Got 52 into the lifeboat and cast off to try and find tug. After searching for some time, and being hit again by a fishing boat, I decided at 0100 to return under my own power to Dover.'

To add to the confusion a dense fog descended on the Channel, and on her passage back to England, the minesweeper *Leda* struck the skoot *Marechal Foch* which sank. *Leda* sustained damage to her bows, but the forward bulkhead held.

E.A. Leppard was the owner of a former 52-foot naval harbour launch *Letitia*, which was normally berthed in Chichester Canal. He had set off from Chichester at 06.00 hours on 2 June, reaching Hythe on the morning of 3 June where a Royal Navy sub-lieutenant and three sailors went on board and took over. The boat's masts were taken down and a machine-gun was fitted to the deck. Mr. Leppard stayed on board as the launch, along with three other yachts, were towed across the Channel by the tug *Sun XV* and he later wrote of his experiences:

'Arrived off Dunkirk at 11.30 p.m. and cast of from tug. Proceeded into Dunkirk past the Mole, and up the Canal for about

Dunkirk fell to the Germans on 4 June 1940, the first German troops entering the town between 07.00 hours and 08.00 hours. Here some of the early occupiers are pictured on the beach beside a camouflaged dug-out with a Union Flag still flying. The wreck in the background is that of the French destroyer *L'Adroit*.

two miles. Moored alongside the quay and proceeded to take troops on board. Could find no Englishmen so took on board forty Frenchmen. Left the quay and proceeded outside the Mole to H.M.S. *Walrus*[5], who took troops on board. Swell from other craft made ship dash into the side of the warship, tearing rails down and breaking ropes. Had orders to load on board about 400lbs of T.N.T., in two barrels. Five naval ratings came on board and proceeded to wreck of H.M.S. *Mosquito*. Went alongside and put on ratings and T.N.T. Waiting there for ratings to fix charge to blow up the wreck. When all was ready naval ratings jumped on board and we got away from the wreck in quick time.'[6]

Mr. Leppard also wrote that artillery shells were exploding all the time *Letitia* was in Dunkirk and off the Mole, the shrapnel

and shell fragments falling all around. With the town of Dunkirk in flames and the explosions overhead there was enough light to see the masts and funnels of the ships that had sunk outside the harbour.

The demolition party Mr. Leppard refers to was from the gunboat *Locust*. Its skipper, Lieutenant Ackroyd Norman Palliser Costobadie, provided a little more detail: 'Demolition party consisting of Lieutenant Holdsworth and 6 men left by Motor boat for wreck of *Mosquito*. On arrival, it was found that the wreck was submerged to the level of the battery deck, and despite repeated efforts of Lieut. Holdsworth who attempted to enter the Captain's Quarters, the forward charge had to be placed in the wheelhouse. The after charge was placed in the after magazine. ▶

German soldiers examine a pile of equipment that was left on the beaches to the east of Dunkirk.

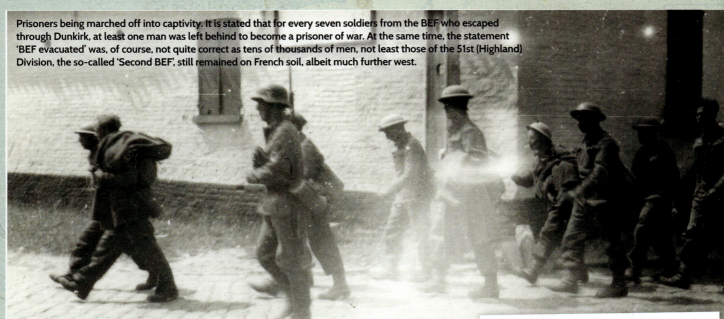

Prisoners being marched off into captivity. It is stated that for every seven soldiers from the BEF who escaped through Dunkirk, at least one man was left behind to become a prisoner of war. At the same time, the statement 'BEF evacuated' was, of course, not quite correct as tens of thousands of men, not least those of the 51st (Highland) Division, the so-called 'Second BEF', still remained on French soil, albeit much further west.

'The demolition party were working under great difficulties due to the movement of the wreck in the swell and to the darkness, and great initiative was displayed by Lieut. Holdsworth in placing the charges which were heavy and difficult to handle, and were somewhat dangerous.

'The demolition party returned on board at 02.05 having fired the charges. The explosion blew off the fore part and after part of the wreck and should have prevented anything of value falling into enemy hands.'[7]

Mick Wenban, a licensed waterman, volunteered to join the Thames steam tug *Challenge*, which had made repeated trips to Dunkirk and on 3 June was back in Dover harbour when the destroyer HMS *Worcester* collided with the passenger ferry SS *Maid of Orleans*. The collision was the result of *Worcester*'s manoeuvrability being severely restricted due to damage to her two screws and her rudder.

At 20.00 hours, *Challenge*, along with the other tugs *Crested Cock*, *Sun VII* and *Sun XIII*, took them in tow, hauling HMS

Worcester to the Prince of Wales Pier. Then at approximately 21.30 hours *Challenge* was ordered to steam back to Dunkirk and 'pick up or rescue anything'. At 23.00 hours, she was off North Goodwin in a line with *Ocean Cock*, *Crested Cock*, *Fairplay I*, *Sun VII*, *Sun XI* and *Sun XII*, all heading towards Dunkirk with the same orders. 'We were under command of a naval officer this time, although the vessel was still under the red ensign,' said Mick Wenban describing that final trip across the Channel. 'When we got there, there was a lot of noise going on from German guns. There were many big fires.'

The great risk the ships faced at Dunkirk was in becoming stranded on the sands. To avoid this, the ships would drop anchor in deep water and then go astern on it, so that the vessel was facing out to sea, ready for a quick getaway.

Challenge was anchored in just such a fashion whilst Captain Parker scanned the shore with his binoculars. Mick Wenban junior recalled what he was told by his father:

Twenty-two of the 'little ships' pass back up the Thames on 9 June 1940 after their involvement in the Dunkirk Evacuation. Only two of the boats can be identified. In the row nearest the camera, second from the right, is the motor yacht *Ryegate II*. She had been commandeered from her owner, a Mr. A. Ryeland of Banstead in Surrey. In the middle of the furthest row, and identified from another image from the same series, is *Rapid 1*.

'He [Charlie Parker] was looking on the quay and he was saying there are all these soldiers there. Mick ask them if they want to step back. So Dad jumped up on the stern of the tug and he was shouting to them on the beach "come on lads we'll take you back" and they all start saying "*Achtung*" and they start firing at them and someone said, "Jesus Christ they're bloody Germans!"'

If the Germans were in Dunkirk Harbour it meant that there were no more Allied troops left to save. 'It was obvious that our little tug could do no more, although we were told to try and bring back anything we could see,' Mick Wenban senior related. 'Our officer eventually ordered the tug back to Dover.' *Challenge* was one of the last vessels to leave Dunkirk.

The Mémorial des Alliés is situated on the Digues des Alliés on the seafront at Dunkirk at the boundary with neighbouring Malo-les-Bains. It was built using stones from a damaged wharf in the harbour.
(Courtesy of Tony Grist)

Almost certainly photographed in the dunes to the east of Dunkirk, such as at Bray, these wooden crosses mark the spot where British casualties, and possibly one French soldier, were buried during Operation *Dynamo*..

It was also on Monday, 3 June 1940, when *Medway Queen* set out on her final voyage of the evacuation. 'Whilst we were in Ramsgate getting ready to go over for that last time', Albert Nason later wrote, 'Lieutenant Cook called the men together and told everyone to write a postcard to their families and then all hands went ashore to the pub on the jetty where the Captain bought us all a drink.' Vice Admiral Ramsay, who was in overall command of Operation Dynamo, ordered that all ships must leave Dunkirk by 02.30 hours the following day.

'We berthed alongside the Mole for the last time at midnight,' remembered Sub Lieutenant Graves. 'Machine-gun fire could be clearly heard. This time we took on about 400 French soldiers, all the BEF had by this time left.'

'A destroyer astern of *Medway Queen* was hit and flung forward onto our starboard paddlebox, extensively damaging the sponson. The Captain nursed us away from the berth with difficulty and the *Medway Queen* made off very slowly down the harbour, with the familiar Mole still lit by blazing oil tanks falling astern.'

In what was a remarkable achievement, the little paddle steamer made a total of seven trips to Dunkirk and back. In the course of these journeys *Medway Queen* and its crew rescued 7,000 soldiers – more than any other

vessel smaller than a destroyer. Captain Cook and Lieutenant Graves each received the DSC, two of her Petty Officers, Crossley and MacAlister, as well as Seaman Olly, were awarded the DSM and two other members of the crew were Mentioned in Despatches.

As the battered little paddle boat limped into Dover, her crew utterly exhausted, the ships in the harbour sounded their sirens and Vice Admiral Ramsey sent the signal, 'Well done *Medway Queen*'!

There was no such rejoicing for the French rear-guard. General Barthélémy hoped to be able to slip away undetected by the Germans soon after nightfall to reach the harbour before midnight. His hopes were dashed, as the French historian Jacques Mordal cuttingly commented, his words being translated by David Devine:

'As he approached Malo with the rearguard, he saw a vast crowd of troops materialize suddenly as the news of the last departure spread. Out of the cellars and the holes, streams of unarmed men appeared, emerging everywhere, converging on the Mole, until they became an immense river of men frozen solid at the approaches. These hidden heroes, these warriors who for days had not left their shelters, had no intention of giving up their chances of escape to those who had been fighting for them.'[8]

Though the Royal Navy destroyer HMS *Shikari* managed to sneak into Dunkirk and take off 600 of Barthélémy's men, the rest of the rear-guard fell into enemy hands. 'No episode in the epic of Dunkirk,' wrote Mordal, 'caused more heartbreak'. ▶

ABOVE: **MTB 102 pictured on the River Thames during Her Majesty Queen Elizabeth II's Diamond Jubilee celebrations in 2012. Launched in May 1937, MTB 102 not only participated in *Dynamo*, but was involved in Operation *Overlord*, thereby seeing both the departure and return of Allied troops to France.** (Courtesy of Mark Longair)

BELOW: **Abandoned vehicles and equipment litter one of the evacuation beaches. Note the abandoned Thames sailing barge, believed to be *Ethel Everard*, in the centre background.**

THE 'MIRACLE' OF DUNKIRK

At 08.00 hours, German troops reached Bastion 32, the French naval headquarters in Dunkirk where General Beaufrère formally surrendered, bringing the fighting to a conclusion. An hour and a half later the Germans were at the foot of the East Mole, which was still packed with helpless French soldiers. The official end of operations against Allied forces at Dunkirk was marked shortly afterwards with the raising of the swastika over the East Mole at 10.20 hours.

Hitler was ecstatic at the news: 'Dunkirk has fallen! 40,000 French and English troops are all that remains of the formerly great armies. Immeasurable quantities of materiel have been captured. The greatest battle in the history of the world has come to an end.'

The truth was that Hitler had failed to prevent the BEF from escaping. It would prove a catastrophic error. On 4 June, no less than 26,175 men were landed back in the UK to make a grand total of 338,226 that had been rescued from France since the 27 May.

A group of the 'Little Ships' is honoured by a formal review as it sails past the saluting base in the peaceful upper reaches of the Thames in July 1940.

This memorial commemorating all those involved in Operation *Dynamo* was unveiled on Dover's seafront, near Waterloo Crescent, by Major-General John Carpenter, the then chairman of the Dunkirk Veterans' Association, on Saturday, 16 August 1975. Major-General Carpenter was a subaltern at Dunkirk in 1940 and in the early hours of 31 May he led his platoon on foot to the beach at Bray Dunes. As there were no ships there, he waded out to an abandoned lifeboat into which he crammed his men. They were machine-gunned by enemy aircraft but were eventually picked up by a Dutch coaster and returned to the UK.

Winston Churchill told the House of Commons that Operation *Dynamo* was 'a miracle of deliverance'. It was achieved, he said, 'by valour, by perseverance, by perfect discipline, by faultless service, by resource, by skill, by unconquerable fidelity, is manifest to us all.

'The enemy was hurled back by the retreating British and French troops. He was so roughly handled that he did not harry their departure seriously. The Royal Air Force engaged the main strength of the German Air Force, and inflicted upon them losses of at least four to one; and the Navy, using nearly 1,000 ships of all kinds, carried over 335,000 men, French and British, out of the jaws of death … Could there have been an objective of greater military importance and significance for the whole purpose of the war than this?[9]

It certainly felt that a victory had been snatched from the jaws of certain defeat. But amidst the relief and the rejoicing was the basic fact that 68,000 men had been killed, wounded, taken prisoner or listed as missing, many of the latter lost in the seas off Dunkirk.

Losses were not confined to men, the BEF having abandoned almost all its equipment. The numbers are staggering. There were 2,472 guns, 20,000 motorcycles, and almost 65,000 other vehicles abandoned, including virtually every one of the 445 tanks sent to France. In addition, 416,000 tons of stores, more than 75,000 tons of ammunition and 162,000 tons of fuel were destroyed or left behind. The RAF also lost 145 aircraft, including forty-two invaluable Spitfires. Total RAF losses for the Battle of France were 959, a number only marginally less than the Battle of Britain which was to follow.[10] It was the heaviest defeat in British history, until the debacle of Singapore in the winter of 1941/42.

Churchill wisely sought to dampen down the widespread jubilation with which *Dynamo* was reported by the press and received by the public. 'We must be very careful not to assign to this deliverance the attributes of a victory,' he told the House. Wars are not won by evacuations.'

Nevertheless, the events of Operation *Dynamo* had, in many ways, brought the nation together as never before or since, and the 'Dunkirk spirit' carried the British people through five further years of war. ✠

NOTES:
1. TNA, ADM 234/360.
2. ibid.
3. TNA, ADM 199/789.
4. BBC Peoples War, W.E. Birtles, *Dunkirk Aged 17*.
5. There was no HMS *Walrus* in Royal Navy service in 1940 and he must have misheard *Locust*.
6. TNA, ADM 334/83.
7. TNA, ADM 199/788A.
8. Devine, pp.219-20.
9. Churchill, *Hansard, House of Commons debate, 04 June 1940 vol. 361, cc787-98*.
10. Sean Longdon, *Dunkirk: The Men They Left Behind* (Constable and Robinson, London, 2009), p.11.

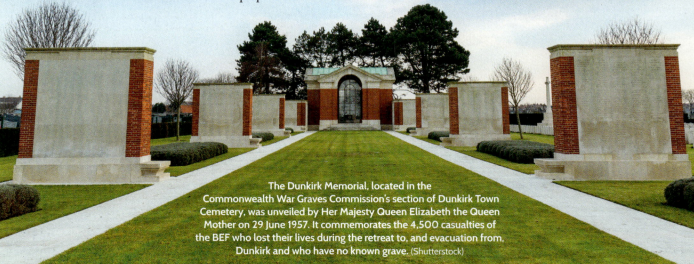

The Dunkirk Memorial, located in the Commonwealth War Graves Commission's section of Dunkirk Town Cemetery, was unveiled by Her Majesty Queen Elizabeth the Queen Mother on 29 June 1957. It commemorates the 4,500 casualties of the BEF who lost their lives during the retreat to, and evacuation from, Dunkirk and who have no known grave. (Shutterstock)